# A Cow In The Pool

## & Udder Humorous Farm Stories

Joe Peck

# A Cow In The Pool
## & Udder Humorous Farm Stories

**Joe Peck**

Illustrations by Andrew R. Taormina

Peckhaven Publishing
178 Wagman's Ridge
Saratoga Springs NY 12866
2001

# A Cow In The Pool
# & Udder Humorous Farm Stories

By Joe Peck
Illustrations by Andrew R. Taormina

Published by:
**Peckhaven Publishing**
178 Wagman's Ridge
Saratoga Springs NY 12866-6620
www.joepeckonline.com
e-mail: joe@joepeckonline.com

International Standard Book Number: 0-9714620-0-3

Library of Congress Control Number: 2001095926

First Edition
Printed in the United States of America

# ACKNOWLEDGEMENTS

This book could not have been written without the patience, sense of humor, and editing skills of my wonderful wife, Pat. Each of our children has made their contribution: Sharon, by lending her publishing and writing experience; Deborah, by offering story ideas; her husband, Sean, for his computer expertise and website design; and David, for allowing me time off from farm chores to pursue my writing avocation.

I also wish to acknowledge my parents, Schuyler and Viola Haas Peck, and my late brother, Lou Peck, for giving me the ability to see what is really important in life. Also, my Aunt Milly Haas Shaw, whose boundless energy, enthusiasm, and wit has sustained me through many a crisis.

Special thanks go to writers Eleanor Jacobs, David Pitkin. and Ron Ferra for their advice and encouragement.

To Dick McGuire, whose special way with words inspired me to put my feelings down on paper, and to Al Lounsbury, who has been an inspiration to me and hundreds of others, thank you for your encouragement.

Thanks also to The Innovative Resources Group for guidance and cover layout and to Andrew R.Taormina for the wonderful caricatures throughout the book. Andrew, a graduate of the State University of New York at Fredonia, holds a Bachelor of Arts Degree in Graphic Design. This book is his first published work.

I also wish to thank the members of Thorobred Toastmasters for letting me try out my story ideas on them. And a special thanks to all the farmers, farm wives, agribusiness people and so many others who have, in one way or another, contributed to the stories in this book.

# INTRODUCTION

Farmers have a tendency to defend their quirky, often austere profession by saying, "Farming is more a way of life than a job." It is that way of life that I have attempted to portray in my writings.

In my lifetime I have seen farming change from a family centered love of land and animals into a large business dependent on narrow margins and critical management decisions. Along the way I learned that the only way we could enjoy our life on the family farm was to relax and not take ourselves too seriously.

I have had the wonderful opportunity to spend my entire life on the farm on which I was born. I have enjoyed experiences that only farm life provides: learning the trade from my father, accepting the challenge of caring for a herd, farmstead and family, proudly watching my son adopt my profession, and realizing that he has become a better manager than me. This and the amazing luck of meeting, falling in love with and marrying one of the most capable and caring individuals I have ever known, and together raising three farm kids, each very successful in their own right, has made me even more dedicated to communicating what life on a farm is really like.

A sense of humor is such a valuable possession. It takes the cry out of a crisis. It makes a cow in the pool a problem to solve rather than a disaster. Take a moment from your stressful life, read these stories, and soon you will see the humor in your life.

# ABOUT THE AUTHOR

Joe Peck, a Cornell University graduate, Certified Toastmaster, and humorous speaker, milks 100 registered Holsteins on Peckhaven Farm in Saratoga County, NY, in partnership with his son, David. The farm is both a Century Farm and a Dairy of Distinction.

An agricultural leader, Joe has been recognized by Cornell University as an outstanding alumni and by the governor of New York State for the contributions that he and his family have made to agriculture and community.

Joe's optimism and sense of humor helped him become a popular speaker, humorist, and accomplished writer of humorous stories about farm life. His writings have appeared in the *American Agriculturist, Agri-Mark Journal,* and *Agricultural News Serving Eastern New York.*

A member of the National Speakers Association and Toastmasters, Joe has been entertaining audiences for years with a combination of enlightened inspiration, homespun yarns, and stand-up comedy, drawn from a lifetime of farm experience.

Joe uses good, clean family-style humor, lives up to his reputation for being funny, and sends people out on a high note, feeling good about themselves.

FOR SCHEDULING INFORMATION:
**Joe Peck**
Peckhaven Farm
178 Wagman's Ridge
Saratoga Springs NY 12866
(518) 584-4129
Joe @joepeckonline.com

# CONTENTS

# Prologue

## A COW IN THE POOL!

On a farm there is good news and there is bad news. The good news includes statements such as, "It's a heifer," "It could have been worse," and "I think we found all the pieces." Bad news sounds like: "Grab the fire extinguisher," "I can't find all the pieces," and, worst of all, "There is a cow in the pool."

Apparently a yearling heifer had jumped over a gate and wandered out of the barn, across the snow covered lawn and unsuspectingly fell right through the pool cover into the icy cold water of our slumbering inground pool. Fortunately, a neighbor had watched the entire drama, as if in slow motion, from her kitchen window. Not being familiar with the buoyancy of the average Holstein, she came toward the barn on a dead run, screaming, "There's a cow in the pool!" Now, that is what I call bad news.

With the serenity of a clergyman in a church full of screaming babies, I calmly told her to relax. Everything would be all right. That's what I said, but inside, I had visions of facing the daunting task of lifting a 600-pound heifer up out of the deep end of an ice-covered swimming pool. What should I do? Dial 911, call the vet, or get out my book on CPR for cows? Then it dawned on me: why attempt the rescue by hand when using a machine could make the task easier, faster and, most important, safer. My son, David, and I quickly raced to get a nylon rope halter and the tractor with the front-end loader. Reaching the pool edge, I found the heifer furiously treading water, her head barely above the icy surface. I deftly placed the halter on her head as David maneuvered the loader bucket. After tying the halter lead to a hook welded to the bucket, I stepped back and watched as David swiftly and easily plucked her from the frigid water. She promptly stood up and shook the water from her fur coat, like a dog emerging from the surf. She couldn't wait to get back to her comrades in the dry free stall heifer barn.

I checked on her that night and, other than being exceptionally clean and white, she looked just like the others in her group who had missed her exciting adventure. It shouldn't happen again as I now have a sign, "No swimming without permission." Surely, there will never be another cow in the pool.

*(But it happened again! Two years later there was another cow in the pool. I guess cows can't read after all.)*

# Chapter 1

## WHAT IS A FARMER?

The modern farmer is a paradox. He is a purchasing agent with too many needs and not enough cash, a production expert faced with a surplus, and a corporate executive fighting a cost-price squeeze. He is an economist trying to defy the law of supply and demand, a mechanic who knows the term 'maintenance-free' means that when it breaks it can't be fixed, and a personnel manager who has learned to be diplomatic or do the work himself.

What is a farmer? Well, it really depends on whom you ask. To his wife, he's a big eater, a sound sleeper, and a worry. To a politician, he's someone to make promises to just before elections; to an agribusiness man, he's a good customer. To his banker, he's a big depositor; to his loan officer he's a checkbook manager who somehow makes his payments on time.

To his neighbors, he's a friend who is always willing to lend a hand. To his children, he is someone who always has time for them, even though they may have to do their chores first. To the grocer, he is a godsend. To his mechanic, he is a wizard at holding things together with twine, wire, and electrician's tape. To his machinery dealer, he is someone with the bargaining skills of a used car salesman and the integrity of a clergyman. To his doctor, he is a physical wonder.

To himself he is protector of God's land and animals with the optimism of an Olympian athlete and the pride of a new parent. He will never tell you that though, because he's too busy to take the time to visit right now. In fact, a fitting epitaph for his tombstone would be: "Not yet, Lord. I've got too much to do."

# YOU MIGHT BE A FARMER IF...

How does anyone know for sure that they were cut out to be a farmer? After farming for what seems like over one hundred years, I have noticed that nearly all farmers have some very similar traits.

You might be a farmer if you can get a good night's sleep in 20 minutes. You might be a farmer if, when you bite into a piece of meat, you can tell what kind of forage the animal was fed. And you might be a farmer if you are baffled by people who eat brunch at 11 a.m. and dinner at 3 p.m.

You might be a farmer if you can deliver a calf, dehorn a cow, lance an abscess, and still have appetite enough to go to the all-you-can-eat spaghetti dinner at school that night.

Yes, you might be a farmer if, on your honeymoon, you stop at every farm machinery dealer you pass or if your idea of a romantic date is a free dinner at the coop annual meeting. You might be a farmer if you can tell from a cow's bellow whether she is calving, in heat, or just hungry; or if you know by heart the serial numbers of all your tractors, but you can't remember the date of your wife's birthday. You might be a farmer if your mailbox post is made out of old cultivator parts or if you know how to pull a calf but not how to change a diaper.

You might be a farmer if you look upon driving the pickup home from town without brakes as a challenge rather than a problem or if there is more oil on your coveralls than in your car. You might be a farmer if you realize that the only reason the grass is always greener on the other side of the fence is because it got more manure than your side. And you might be a farmer if you can fix almost anything with baler twine, a jackknife, and duct tape or if there are more seed corn hats on your walls than pictures.

You might be a farmer if you wear your barn clothes to the supermarket just so everyone will let you through the checkout line first.

You might be a farmer if you frequently take a different route to town, just to check on the neighbor's crops or if you have the tools and parts in your pickup to help a stranded motorist get back on the road. And you might be a farmer if you are the only person who is happy when it rains on the weekend.

But the best way to tell if you might be a farmer is if you enjoy a John Deere calendar more than a Hooter's calendar.

# REAL FARMERS

With so many people moving to the country now, it is getting harder and harder to tell who the real farmers are. Here are some clues.

Real farmers don't make pets out of anything they can eat and they don't wear L.L. Bean boots.

Real Farmers don't jog. If you do see them running, probably they accidentally stepped in a hornet's nest.

Real farmers never walk in the rain, but they do drive tractors in the rain, snow and bitter cold.

They don't drink diet soda or two percent milk or eat tofu.

Real farmers don't flinch when they snap on the jumper cables nor buy their Christmas trees at super markets.

And they never stack their firewood higher than their wife can reach.

Real farmers tow their kicker wagons home on the state road at 50 mph or faster because they know if they go any slower some fool will try to pass them.

Real farmers have no respect for mailmen who are late, milk truck drivers who are early and milk inspectors who are on time.

Real farmers don't trust the weatherman, but listen to him daily anyway.

Real farmers despise stepped on teats, clogged fuel filters, and temperamental baler knotters.

They look forward to spring, a day off, and a warm gentle rain, but only after baling the last bale.

They hate power failures at chore time, salesmen at mealtime, and nosy neighbors who ask, "Just how much did that cost?"

Real farmers are driven by a deep sense of pride in everything they do and the blind hope that next year will be better than this year has been so far.

# ARE FARMERS HELPLESS IN THE KITCHEN?

Too often farmers are accused of being able to do almost anything, except prepare their own meals. This criticism is unfair and, in most cases, untrue. In fact, farmers have learned, out of necessity, to prepare a meal of great variety and taste in record time.

Recently, upon returning from the barn, I found a note taped to the microwave from the person who usually prepares my meals, which said, "Gone shopping. Get your own supper."

Rising to the occasion, I began my meal with an old favorite of graham crackers spread with half an inch of a peanut butter and jelly mixture, imbedded with tiny marshmallows, and cemented in place with a second graham cracker.

This delicious morsel should always be accompanied with cold milk served in a wide mouth jelly glass. This is essential so that the entire confection can be dipped into the milk to soften it for eating. Timing is critical for if it is held in the milk too long, the soaked portion could break off on the way to the mouth and fall onto the kitchen floor. If that happens, simply kick it under the nearest cabinet so no one will see it. Needless to say, it is best to bring the mouth to the jelly glass. This concoction has the added advantage of providing something from each of the four food groups: fat, cholesterol, sugar and preservatives.

For the meat, I chose my favorite - hotdogs. Simply place two hotdogs on a plate in the microwave and cook on high for two minutes. If the hotdogs are really cheap, this should provide a tasty treat as well as some picturesque sculptured shapes resembling miniature logs that had exploded.

Since I eat almost anything but green vegetables, I skipped this course entirely. For the fruit I selected tinned pears, which unfortunately slipped from my spoon and fell to the floor. After blotting with a paper towel to remove the cat hairs, I dipped the pear lightly in hotdog relish to compensate for the loss of pear syrup, creating a unique flavor.

I topped off my meal with a package of Oreo cookies, which I crushed into a bowl of two-day-old chocolate pudding that I found in the refrigerator. It was beautiful. To ease my conscience, I washed all this down with two bottles of diet Pepsi without caffeine.

So, you see, we farmers are not helpless in the kitchen. That is, not until it's time to clean up the mess we've made.

# SKILL

Some people have a natural talent that makes what they do look so easy that anyone could do it. Skill, on the other hand, is a high degree of proficiency or expertness that comes from training and practice. A farmer must learn many skills to survive in such a perilous profession.

Skill is convincing the greatest gossip in the county that the secret to our high milk production is exposing our cows to classical music 24 hours a day.

Skill is convincing the repairman that the machine simply stopped working without warning, when, in reality, you were always in too much of a hurry to grease it.

Skill is getting a cow to eat more, simply by devising a way for her to think that she is stealing it.

Skill is opening a chain stitch on a bag of feed without cutting yourself.

Skill is convincing your wife that you don't have time to mow the lawn, but yet have time to go to an auction.

Skill is making an unpleasant job sound so exciting and challenging that someone else will do it for you.

Skill is getting both an insulated vest and a jacket out of a seed corn salesman before finally giving him an order.

Skill is getting your computer to do what you want it to do without locking up, losing its memory, or catching fire.

Skill is not losing any of the bills that come in the mail between milk checks.

Skill is persuading the parts person at the dealership that your crisis is much more important than that of the farmer on the phone.

Skill is crossing a narrow bridge with a wide haybine without slowing down.

Ineptness is getting the tractor and manure spreader so stuck in the mud that there is nothing sticking out but the steering wheel.

Skill is getting your son to believe it wasn't your fault.

And **real** skill is getting the tractor and manure spreader unstuck before your neighbors notice.

# MORE SCENTS THAN SENSE

Like most farmers, whenever I'm away from the farm I can't wait to get back to see if everything is all right. This used to entail a time-consuming walk around, a mini-inspection, just to monitor the progress of chores, fieldwork, and coffee breaks. Now I can gather just as much information quickly and easily simply by using the ultimate secret weapon, my well-developed sense of smell.

That's right, so much can be learned about a farm just by analyzing the mixture of odors permeating any farmyard. A slight breeze from the direction of the barn also helps. For example, a strong corn silage or haylage aroma tells me that the cows have just been fed, whereas a burning clutch smell indicates the mixer wagon may have had difficulty mixing that last load. A manure smell means that the barn was just cleaned. A strong manure smell says that they cleaned the heifer barn, too. The scent of wood smoke means that the stove has been filled; the smell of hydraulic oil indicates that a hose has ruptured.

Some odors bring good news, like the wonderful aroma of newly mown hay, fresh sawdust and even wet paint. Others indicate, decidedly, bad news. No one likes the smell of burning rubber, calf scours or sweaty socks. Exhaust fumes, although not pleasant, at least tell you that engines are running and presumably doing their jobs. I like the good smells best.

Sometimes it is hard to sort out all of these odors; they mingle so easily with many other scents you would rather be inhaling. My favorite is lilacs in blossom or apple pie straight from the oven. Actually, if it were fresh pie that I smelled, I would rather stop and have a piece right away and then worry about what might have happened while I was away.

# INQUIRING MIND

Methodically moving my herd of cows into the holding area where they would await milking, I was suddenly aware of nearly one hundred pairs of eyes intently watching my every move.

I wonder if that is how a teacher feels walking into a full classroom for the first time - all those inquiring minds seeking answers to so many questions. For a cow the questions are limited in both scope and number. They are seeking answers to practical rather than theoretical questions on the order of: "Will this take long?" or "When I finally get into the parlor, will the power go off?" and "Will there be fresh feed waiting for me when I leave the milking parlor?"

These are easy questions to answer, if only they wouldn't keep asking them at every milking. Oh, I know cows can't talk, but I can see the concern in their eyes. It doesn't matter to them that they still have the same questions.

I'm beginning to understand why it takes so much patience to be a good teacher. They, too, must answer the same questions over and over, as well as teach the same lessons repeatedly. Of course, cows don't talk about you behind your back or get a laugh out of imitating you in front of their friends.

I think that the farmer, however, has the advantage since there are no tests to administer, papers to correct, or parents to impress. A teacher, on the other hand, gets a new crop of minds each September, can take a break every weekend, and use the same exams from last year but just change the answers.

I guess I would rather work with cows than kids. Cows don't talk back nor whisper to each other in the back of the room or pass notes. It's just too bad farmers don't get all summer off, too, so they could renew their energy and spirits for the year ahead.

# LISTS

Management experts claim that farmers could make better use of their time, if only they would prioritize their daily goals by making a simple list, with the most important jobs at the top.

Taking their advice, I make a list everyday of all the things I want to get done that day. I rarely do any of them. That doesn't mean I do nothing, for most days I accomplish a lot. It's just that farming doesn't lend itself to clear-cut, easily defined tasks.

For example, do you put down obvious things like "do chores" or "fix burst pipe in the milk house" when it is apparent that these things must get done whether they are on the list or not? Or do your include major projects which take more than one day to accomplish? I don't because I'm too intimidated to even begin such monumental tasks.

Actually, the hardest part is just making the list. Once completed with enough items to fill the page, the next biggest obstacle is deciding which item to do first. You should never do the first item first. That would be like accepting the first price the salesman gives you when dickering on a new car. The more you stare at your list, the more you realize you are fast becoming a slave to it. Unfortunately, all of the items look too formidable, too complicated, or too messy to get into right now. It is as if the list were mocking you by just laying there whispering, "Go ahead, make my day!"

By now it is lunchtime, so I always put the list aside until after lunch when I'll be energized to go at it in earnest. Later, if I'm lucky, something will come up that must be done immediately, like pulling a calf, fixing a hydraulic leak or going to the bathroom, which distracts me momentarily from deciding which items on the list I will attack first.

A word of warning here. If you are not careful, when the time comes to look back over the major accomplishments of the day, there may not be any. This is when you start thinking about your list for tomorrow. Since my desk is cluttered with past daily lists, perhaps I should start making my lists on paper that will self-destruct in 24 hours.

# FARMERS ARE LUCKY

When I view the activities of over 98 percent of the American population who are not farming, I cannot help but feel a bit sad. That's right, it is sadness I feel, not envy. Sadness because there are so many of life's joys that they will never experience. Sadness because, while they think they are having a good time, a farmer somewhere is having even more fun.

Take weekends for example. The average suburban family sleeps late on Saturday mornings wasting valuable time, while a farmer has witnessed the sunrise, done a day's work, and either saved a life or averted a crisis before most people are brewing their morning coffee and making chore lists for their spouse. Yes, a farmer has a much more interesting and rewarding life. What a shame more people can't share these joys with him.

Vacations are another area where farmers have the advantage. A family vacation for most people involves traveling hundreds of miles in a vehicle covered with bikes, canoes, and ice chests, and crammed with noisy kids, stuffed toys, and musty sleeping bags. A farmer, on the other hand, need only visit another farm, tour the lot of a machinery dealer. or attend an auction, to feel renewed, without even missing a milking. He has avoided a wasted week of torn tents, burnt food, and zillions of black fly bites.

Farmers also have the advantage when it comes to doing chores around the house. While most Americans are manicuring lawns, resealing blacktop driveways, and cleaning out garages, a farmer is always too busy milking, mowing, or making hay, to be bothered with such frivolous activities.  After all, he must find a way to feed the world and still have time to look busy when unannounced visitors drop by.

Farmers also avoid costly lunches just to impress prospective clients.  Instead, farmers usually grab a simple sandwich and an apple, to be gulped down while bouncing along on a dusty tractor.  And then there are sports, another waste of time.  While many people participate in a variety of sports. farmers get great pleasure from watching a neighbor's tractor being pulled from the mud, without the cost of cable TV or stadium tickets.

It is simply amazing how much of life one misses by not living on a farm.

# FARMERS ARE DIFFERENT

It is hard to explain just how farmers are different from everyone else, but they are. Maybe it is just that they have different priorities than most folks. Their fierce dedication to their profession allows them little time for pursuits common to others.

That is why farmers never have time to rake leaves but always have time to go to an auction. Or why chores are always more important than visiting the in-laws.

Farmers do take time to shop for Christmas presents for their wives, but usually forget where they hid them until about the middle of March.

Farmers love their families but measure time in relation to events on the farm. For example, if you ask a farm wife, "When did you build the heifer barn?" she will say, "Let me think a minute. It was the year Scott was born and he was seven in August."

Ask a farmer the same question and he is apt to say, "It was the year we bought the big tractor, and she's just seven years old now."

Because a farmer is expected to be a combination mechanic, veterinarian, accountant, electrician, agronomist, plumber, and carpenter all rolled into one, sometimes he should be forgiven for being oblivious to lawns that need mowing, doors that sag, and bath tubs that need scrubbing.

But, in spite of his shortcomings, today's American farmer provides enough food and fiber for 128 people, 94 in the United States and 34 abroad. Yes, he is different and we are all better for it.

# REAL FARM WIVES

Being a farm wife is one of the most challenging roles any woman could accept. Real farm wives must learn some survival skills; most learn them the hard way.

A real farm wife NEVER talks during the weather report, nor asks, "How is your day going?" when she knows the milk inspector just left.

A real farm wife never expects to get anywhere on time and doesn't mind dropping off a bull calf at the livestock market on her way to a parent teacher conference.

She has to learn to keep the chain from going slack when being towed and be able to pull her jeans on over her nightgown, slip into her boots, and be out the door in less than 30 seconds when awakened in the middle of the night by the dreaded cry, "The cows are out!"

Real farm wives hate it when everyone is late for meals and when salesmen ask, "Is the boss around?"

She is expected to bale all afternoon on a cabless tractor without complaining and still fix supper for the entire 4-H judging team that evening.

A real farm wife must, when faced with a choice between purchasing a new sofa or a monitor for the corn planter, give in, realizing the necessity of accurate seed population even though her sofa looks like a buffalo that has been dead for some time.

She knows, when going for parts, that she must have the year, make, model and serial number of the machine and know, in advance, the answer to any question the most sadistic parts man could ask.

A real farm wife realizes she is the glue that holds the farm and the family together. She knows her own inner satisfaction is probably all the thanks she will ever get.

# ARE YOU A WORKAHOLIC?

While prying my mud-soaked shoes from my bone-weary feet after a 16-hour day, typical for a farmer, I quickly stole a glance at what our town laughably calls a daily paper. There it was, on the first page of the second section, right in the spot reserved for those who aren't really interested in the news, a headline that read: "Are You a Workaholic?"

I had never thought about it before. Maybe I am a workaholic. After all, most farmers are, or they are not farming for long. The article was followed by a questionnaire to help you decide whether or not you are a workaholic. A quick glimpse answered that question for me, once and for all.

For example, how can a farmer honestly answer "no" to questions like, "Do you work more than 40 hours a week?" or "Do you take on extra work because you are concerned it won't otherwise get done?" or "Do you get impatient with people who have other priorities besides work?" There were 20 such questions, almost all of which I could easily answer with a "yes" and only five yeses out of 20 would make me either a workaholic or on my way to becoming one.

Wait a minute. Are farmers really workaholics or is the compulsion to work necessary for them to succeed at farming? I'll let you decide.

1. Have your family and friends given up expecting you on time?

2. Do you get more excited about plowing, planting, and harvesting than spending time with family or friends?

3. Is the activity you like to do best and talk about most some phase of farming?

4. During meals do you find yourself reading, opening mail, or driving a tractor?

5. Even when things are going well, do you constantly worry about what will go wrong next?

6. Do you think about your farm while driving, falling asleep, or when others are talking?

If you answered yes to any of the above questions, congratulations. There is a good chance you are both a workaholic and a farmer.

# COCKTAIL PARTIES

There I was at this cocktail party, feeling like a fish out of water. I don't even drink. Alcohol, that is. Must be a throwback to my strict Baptist upbringing. I had been invited by some of my new neighbors. You know the type, new rural residents with expensive houses and good jobs. It soon became obvious that I was the token farmer giving them a tie to the community they had just adopted.

I thought I was doing just fine, nibbling at what tasted like bait while making small talk with a bunch of svelte yuppies. Then it happened. An emaciated professional woman, lecturing me about the evils of animal fats while munching on some cheese and crackers, suddenly looked me straight in the eye and asked, "And what do you do for a living?"

I was shocked. What could I say? I couldn't admit that I was a dairy farmer. I couldn't let her know it was I who held up her BMW while pulling those heavy loads of haylage home at 12 miles per hour or confess that those smelly loads of manure actually came from my cows.

I panicked. I couldn't lie about my occupation. I had too much pride for that. There was no way out. I had to tell the truth. Finally, after a long period of soul searching (about eight seconds), I assumed an air of confidence and calmly replied, "I'm an animal trainer."

"Oh," she replied, "That must be fascinating. What kind of animals do you train?"

Looking both ways, I leaned toward her as if I were about to reveal a state secret and whispered, "I can't say, but I can tell you that it involves crowding small groups of large animals into a confined space for the purpose of extracting precious nutritional fluids from them."

I assured her it was very strenuous and dangerous work, calling for nerves of steel and the patience of Job. Amazingly, she bought it, especially the part about how difficult it was to train them to lay in individual cubicles at night.

After sharing that revelation with her, I felt right at home with those accomplished, successful, and gullible party guests. I became the hit of the party. I hope she never finds out what I really do for a living or where cheese comes from and what it contains.

# SURVIVAL SECRETS

Farmers are the most misunderstood people in the world, perhaps because theirs is a vocation that sells wholesale but buys retail. It is hard to understand how anyone could choose to produce a product that is perishable, is highly dependent on the weather, and often is sold before the selling price is known. I am not saying that farmers are crazy; it is just that they sometimes are hard to fathom.

Take a common situation in which farmers often find themselves. This mostly wintertime phenomenon occurs when farmers are attending some sort of crowded gathering. It could be a farm meeting sponsored by Cooperative Extension or Farm Bureau, a church service, or even a family reunion. After sitting for a while inside a warm building, most farmers will appear to start to, how shall we say, doze off. Now to the speaker, clergy or family matriarch, this may appear to be rude and insensitive behavior. This is not the case at all.

We have to remember the many frustrations, oops, I mean challenges, which that farmer has had to face that day before he rushed into the house, cleaned up, changed, and sped off to this crowded event. It might have been anything from frozen pipes to jelled fuel filters or even a surprise visit from the milk inspector, but whatever it was, many times the only way to achieve the same state of relaxation as the other attendees is to employ a strategy known as 'relaxation therapy.'

To the untrained eye this appears to be simply snoozing, or to put it more crudely, falling asleep. This is a vast oversimplification of what actually happens. In reality, this is a technique that many farmers have perfected to let their memories select only the good things to remember and let all the bad things simply disappear. It can only be achieved when the body relaxes and slows down to the point that the mind can sort out the farmer's thoughts. Thus, it dumps the sorrows, like the memory of how cold his hands were during the morning milking, and replaces them with the joy of seeing the newborn heifer calf have a healthy appetite.

So the next time you see a farmer's head begin to nod, rest assured he is not tuning you out. Rather, he is engaging in relaxation therapy. It often is the only way farmers can reconcile themselves to a vocation so challenging that only those skilled at this revolutionary technique can succeed.

# FARMER'S REPUTATION

With less than two percent of Americans now living on farms, I often wonder what kind of reputation the American farmer really has. I got my answer on a recent trip through Indiana in a yellow rental truck carrying all of my daughter's possessions home from a two year masters degree-earning stint at the University of Wisconsin. By the time I reached the Indiana turnpike I had become a seasoned trucker, shouting into my CB, "Hey, good buddy!" to all the semi's as they rolled past. After all, the Indiana prairie wasn't much of a challenge after the bumper-hugging traffic of Milwaukee and Chicago.

Cruising at a comfortable 65 miles per hour, I suddenly heard sirens and saw flashing lights behind me. My first thought was, "I can't be speeding as I can't get the darned truck to go over 65."

After I stopped, a very polite man in blue asked me to please step around to the rear of the truck. Then he asked to see my New York driver's license with its unflattering 'deer-caught-in-the-headlights' photo of me on it. After studying it and me, he began to ask a series of questions designed to test my reactions under pressure. First, he asked me where I was going and what I had in the truck. For a few seconds, I entertained the idea of telling him a long story about how it was full of fertilizer and diesel fuel and how I hated the federal government, but then I thought this was neither the time nor the place to find out how handcuffs felt. I simply told him it was full of household goods destined for storage in my garage. Next, he asked if there were any drugs in the Saratoga area. I said, "Probably," since drugs seem to be everywhere, even more available than a McDonald's quarter-pounder.

Then he came right out and asked me, "Are there any drugs in that truck?" I truthfully said, "No, but if you give me a half hour to figure out how to get the combination lock open, I could prove it to you."

"No, no," he replied, "That won't be necessary." Then he looked at my license again, then at me and asked the one question I had been dreading, "What do you do for a living, Mr. Peck?"

I swelled my chest and said proudly, "I'm a dairy farmer." A 'why-didn't-you-say-so earlier' look came over his face and very apologetically he gushed, "Sorry we bothered you, Mr. Peck. You've got enough problems now. You are free to go. Just watch your speed, we want you to get home safely."

I hope this means that the good reputation of the American farmer is still intact. This policeman knew that being a farmer is one occupation no one lies about.

# Chapter 2

## THE DAIRY COW

The dairy cow, once a rangeland creature depending solely on grasses to provide only enough milk for her young. has evolved, through genetic progress, into an animal with the strength and stamina to stand in a holding area for hours, be jostled by animals larger than herself, be goaded into a milking parlor, and still muster the resources necessary to defecate all over you clean coveralls.

With a tongue of sandpaper, she meets the challenge of keeping four stomachs happy with only one mouth. She routinely produces over 100 pounds of milk daily on feeds unfit for human consumption. Her schedule revolves around eating, drinking, chewing her cud and whatever they do to her in the milking parlor.

She produces 200 quarts of methane daily without exploding, and is agile enough to step on her own teats, clever enough to find an open gate in the dark, yet stubborn enough to avoid the parlor door in the broad daylight.

She asks little from life, just a warm dry stall, plenty to eat and drink, and the opportunity to kick somebody once in a while.

This miracle of modern breeding knows what time it is without a clock, is capable of flinching at the sight of a balling gun or a hypodermic needle, and can be depended on to mess the entire length of a clean milking parlor.

In her bovine benevolence she has no respect for social class, veterinarians schedules or parlor cleanliness. It is obvious we just don't appreciate this magnanimous provider of so much food and glue.

# PRE-DIPPING

My county agent, in his infinite wisdom, encouraged us to start "pre-dipping," a method of sanitizing the cows teat ends before milking, practiced by successful dairymen everywhere. The benefits are supposed to be better quality milk that should lead to greater milk production per cow. So far it has led to longer milking time and my face and glasses constantly spattered with a red liquid that stains. However, it is good to have freckles again!

The second biggest problem is finding just the right cup to use to "dip" each teat. Most of the ones on the market were conceived by former mall-rats, who, after four years of partying at a big name university, have become instant plastic designers. It is easy to tell that they have never seen a cow before, let alone an udder.

After each cow is "dipped," each, uh, thing must be wiped dry with an individual paper towel, another costly practice. Fortunately, a more economical way has been found, thanks to my frugal (read cheap) dairy-farming brother in Vermont. He uses newspapers. That's right, we are wiping the cows' udders with newspapers.

Don't laugh, those of us old enough to remember the outhouse can well attest to the absorbency of newsprint. Also, wiping with pieces of newspaper allows you to catch up on last week's news while performing an otherwise boring task. One warning though, this practice could increase your milking time considerably, especially if you should run across an editorial you agree with or worse yet, a question and answer column by Dr. Ruth.

Although I do value my county agent's advice, sometimes the view is different in an air-conditioned office than it is from a noisy, odoriferous and bustling milking parlor. I guess that's the difference between agriculture and farming. Agriculture is talking about it, while farming is actually doing it.

# BEET PULP

I guess I'm not very progressive. It took me over 30 years to go from 20 to 100 cows. Now people do that in a weekend. Those early years with the 20 - 30 cow dairy were great learning experiences. I was brought up on the farm and, like most new college graduates, I thought I knew everything. But I sure learned a lot those first few years. I guess it's what you learn after you know it all that counts.

Take the winter of 1963-64. 1 had gotten the cow numbers up to 40 and had put an addition on the barn. That was the year of a fairly severe drought. We didn't get enough rain all summer to lay the dust. Hay crop was short. Silage crop was even shorter. If we were very, very careful we would have enough roughage to last until mid March.

There were a lot of alternative feeds available. One was beet pulp. I successfully negotiated a deal to buy 5 tons of it. I even paid cash. If I fed a small amount of beet pulp per cow in addition to the silage and hay that I had on hand, it would extend my roughage, the cows ought to milk pretty good, and I would survive at least until pasture season.

The beet pulp came in heavy paper bags, which I carefully stacked in the barn. I will never forget the first day that I started to feed beet pulp. I got out one of those big brown paper bags, carefully undid the chain stitch and meticulously put a small pile of it in front of each cow. If you have never seen beet pulp it looks like the stuff you get out of your pencil sharpener, only much crisper. It is gray in color, certainly not appetizing to humans. The cows all looked at it, sniffed it, pushed it around, and sneezed onto it. After an hour or two nobody had even taken a lick of it.

Here I had five tons of it and the cows weren't even going to sample it. Talk about a sinking feeling. So I fed the silage on top of it. This went on for two or three days. Pretty soon somebody had courage enough to taste it. By the end of the week they were eating it fairly well. After two weeks whenever I got out one of those big brown paper bags every eye was watching me. They could not wait to dive into it.

It was really just a matter of acceptance. They had to get used to the fact that that was all there was. Sort of like kids and kale. But they got used to it and they loved it and they ate it, all five tons. So whenever I run into a situation where the cows won't eat a new feed, I know it is just a matter of time until they accept the fact that that's all there is.

# MY BEST COW

My best cow was sick and I was heart-broken. At last I had a cow, which, at the end of this lactation, would be the envy of all my neighbors, and this morning she was off feed, gaunt, and totally listless. The vet carefully examined her, thumping her sides with his thumb while listening intently with his stethoscope and doing obscene things with his thermometer.

With a voice laden with sadness I said, "I think she is sick because she worries too much. I know she worries about acid rain and its effects on our forests, about the gradual loss of the ozone layer and its effects on global agriculture, and about the solid waste crisis facing so many municipalities today."

The vet said, "No, that isn't it at all. Your cow just has a bad case of indigestion." He proceeded to give her four immense red pills, each one the size of a small dog, and assured me she would be fine in the morning.

As if by magic, the next morning my best cow was fine. I was ecstatic as she waddled into the milking parlor, the old cud chewing, udder bulging, walking appetite she had always been.

Now I don't feel so good. It feels just like there is a chocolate chip cookie lodged crossway in my pancreas. Also, I've been worrying a lot about acid rain, the ozone layer, and the solid waste crisis. I guess it's my destiny to do the worrying for my cows so they can be free to produce milk without a care in world.

# GIVING A COW A PILL

The vet handed me the big jar of boluses and, with a sly smile, casually said, "Just give her four of these twice a day and she should perk right up." Easy for him to say I thought.

Giving a cow a pill is not as easy as it sounds. In the first place, cow pills are very large. They are called boluses just to impress you. By very large I mean the size of a bar of soap cut in half lengthwise. To get a cow to swallow one of these, a balling gun must be used. I say must because there is no other way. This device allows you to insert the pill way down into the mysterious depths of a cow's throat without the ever-present risk of having her defiantly spit the pill back in your face.

It's easy to do. Simply insert the pill into the balling gun, back toward the cow, and with one hand reach over her nose and into her mouth in the spot where her teeth aren't, and, while both hugging her and pressing on the roof of her mouth, simply insert the balling gun until it almost disappears. Press the plunger and she will swallow the pill with one gulp. That's all there is to it!

Almost! If you must give her three more pills and one hand is holding her mouth open, and one hand is holding the balling gun, how do you insert the next pill into the gun? I don't know either. Why don't you ask the vet? This whole thing was his idea anyway.

## A MENU FOR COWS

Having just dined at a fine gourmet restaurant whose menu contained many imaginative adjectives to describe otherwise ordinary food, I found myself staring at the total mixed ration which I had just unloaded into the cows' feed bunk. It was really just ordinary cow feed, but perhaps it could be jazzed up with a more appealing description. Would the cows eat it any better if I told them:

"This morning you are being served an appetizing blend of finely chopped silages, made from the tallest hi-bred corn plants, the leafiest alfalfas and the finest orchard and native grasses, all grown on our own rich mineral soils and harvested with loving care by family members. This tantalizing mixture is further enriched by the addition of soybean oil meal, toasted to a golden brown, and rich, dark distillers dried grains, a by-product of the brewing process of the finest distilled liquors. To further enhance the flavor and to guarantee a nutritionally balanced diet, this mixture has been lightly garnished with high quality sodium bicarbonate, yeast culture, calcium carbonate, selenium and, of course, the finest livestock salt."

Actually, it doesn't make much difference to a cow how you describe her chow, since all she cares about is its palatability, freshness, and prompt delivery. My cows have been getting this same mixture twice a day for over a year, but as I let them return to the bunk to attack this latest batch of total mixed ration, I could almost hear them say, in the voice of an excited child, "OH BOY, SILAGE AGAIN!"

# COW MEMORIES

Always seeking ways to hone my cow care skills, I came across an article recently on how to improve milk production by handling cows more gently. It seems that tame cows give more milk and cows fearful of people are less productive.

What makes a cow fearful? Well, this article contends that cows have excellent memories for both good and bad experiences. Boy, is that hard to believe! Any animal that forgets all about her own calf within three days cannot be classified as having an excellent memory.

This article goes on to say that since animals do not have language, they store their memories like pictures in a photo album or as short bits of audiotape. In the first place, I don't know how anyone could possibly know this for sure. Secondly, there are lots of photo albums I would like to selectively destroy.

Don't get me wrong. I do not doubt this scientific theory that fear memories are located in a part of the brain called the amygdata which is the lower more primitive part of the brain under the cortex. I just can't fathom the notion that a cow has enough memory to recollect what happened her first day in the milking parlor.

The author feels cows will be more productive if we understand that cows do not recognize human faces, but do recognize places, smells, voices, distinctive clothing and certain objects. Therefore we should wear clothing or an apron of one color when milking and another color or funny hat when doing anything that might cause the animal any discomfort. Thus, your cows will associate the comfortable, secure milking process with a yellow apron and give more milk, while they will associate other uncomfortable but necessary treatments with a funny blue hat. I don't know if the cows will remember the funny blue hat the next time, but I certainly will.

It really is disappointing to find out that cows don't recognize faces. I guess the way they perk up as I walk toward them in just their way of saying, "Here comes old dirty sweatshirt again."

# MURPHY'S LAW FOR COWS

Have you ever noticed that the higher producing the cow is, the greater the chance she will get a teat stepped on? Have you ever finished milking exceptionally early only to find that the holding area gate came open and half the herd didn't get milked? Perhaps at the time you realized that something was afoot, some universal principles were just out of your grasp, itching to be called by name. These widely accepted axioms are often referred to as Murphy's Laws and are typified by the statement, "Whatever can possibly go wrong will."

You may not realize that such laws exist for cows, too. Here are some I have been able to identify, but if you have cows, by now you must have some of your own.

LAW #1 - When two cows are due on the same day, the one left out in the free stall area will always freshen before the one you put in the well bedded box stall.

LAW #2 - When sorting cattle, the one you want will always be cut off by the one you don't want.

LAW #3 - The cows are always down on milk on test day.

LAW #4 - The breeder only calls in early on the days you call in late.

LAW #5 - If your wife insists that you finish chores early for a special event, either the motor will burn up on the vacuum pump or some catastrophe will force you to call the vet.

PECK'S COROLLARY: If there is no deadline, chores will be uneventful and you will finish right on schedule.

LAW #6 - The wetter the lawn, the greater the chance the cows will get out during the night.

Now you may think these laws are of a pessimistic nature but nothing could be further from the truth.  Just remember the basic credo of Murphy's Law believers:

*The Optimist believes we live in the best of all possible worlds.  The Pessimist fears this is true.*

# WHY COWS CHEW CUDS

As a public service, I have taken on the task of answering one of the most important questions facing dairy farmers today. That's right, at last you are about to find out why cows have so much time to just stand around and chew gum.

Oh, I know it's not really gum that they are chewing so placidly. It is just that they look happier than an eighth grader with a mouth full of Wrigley's Spearmint. We all know they are just masticating the feed they consumed earlier, but were in too much of a hurry to chew at the time. Sounds like a stupid system, doesn't it? Not really.

Like deer, buffalo and, of all things, the camel, the dairy cow has four stomachs, allowing her to consume large amounts of low energy, high fiber foods very rapidly, the same way vegetarians do. The cow's first stomach, the rumen, is a barrel-like gurgling vat of bacteria, enzymes and other yucky things with the ability to produce proteins and vitamins during the process of breaking down feeds that are not usable by humans. Then the cow or other ruminant, at her leisure, proceeds to regurgitate in small "cuds" this processed glop and chew it thoroughly. From there it goes merrily through the other three stomachs on its way to the manure spreader.

Now, did God design this system so these beautiful animals could produce so much meat, milk and glue merely by grazing on plants that humans couldn't or wouldn't eat or just to give them something to do? Personally I think that this digestive system evolved over centuries in animals with the ability to sneak out of the woods long enough to gobble down enough grass for nourishment before being seen and eaten by a lion or shot by a hunter. This may explain why cows literally jump at any opportunity to get out. They are merely acting upon their instinct to survive. I'm convinced that the cows we are milking today are the descendants of a long line of rapid eaters and fast runners.

# GENES AND GERMS

One of the greatest developments in the scientific world in the twentieth century is genetic engineering. By tinkering with genes, germs, and other stuff, great advances can now be made in animal productivity, longevity, and stupidity.

For example, the never-ending problem of handling dairy cattle waste (manure) can now be solved. Yes, genetic engineering may free dairy farmers from one of the most expensive, offensive, and odoriferous jobs on the farm.

Scientists, by using funny-looking gadgets in laboratories, can now introduce genes from one organism into another. This must be done with utmost care or one could wind-up with boneless chickens, turkeys that baste themselves, or pigs with mustaches.

I am referring, of course, to the crowning achievement of combining the best characteristics of cows and cats into a super animal capable of keeping itself clean, keeping the farm free of rats and mice, and burying its own manure.

This may not be as easy as it sounds. Mother Nature does not like to be tampered with, so there is always the danger of producing a cow that sleeps 14 hours a day, runs away from home for days at a time and is hard to coax down from trees. The idea does have merit, however, so I have decided to apply for a government grant to study the concept further. I figure for a couple million dollars, within two years from my laboratory in Hawaii, I could come up with a detailed plan for an in-depth study of this important scientific break through. Although problems like what to do with the huge hair balls they might cough up or how to keep them from jumping into your lap need to be solved, having a cow that can clean up spilled milk, purr when contented, and sun itself on window sills would certainly be worth the trouble.

# FIVE-DAY COW

We all long for a five-day cow, capable of contentedly producing large volumes of milk Monday through Friday and then, as if by magic, just taking a long nap until Monday morning. A whole herd of such marvelous animals would at last give dairy farmers their weekends off to rest, relax, and recreate, just like their non-farm neighbors. Just think, no more missed football games, no more rushing through milking just to be late for church, no more excuses for not being able to go to quilt shows with the family. Yes, a five-day cow would be a dream come true for most dairy farmers, milk truck drivers, and milking machine repairmen.

Is such an animal possible? The answer is a good strong maybe. You see, once every millennium an unexplainable genetic fluke appears to create a whole new breed within an existing species of animal. The Morgan horse is a good example. All Morgan horses are descended from one superior animal with the ability to pass those traits to its offspring. This same principle must be at work, producing that new breed of disappearing woodchucks. When I'm mowing I see lots of woodchucks, but all I have to do is grab a rifle and those loathsome critters have all disappeared. The same thing happens to deer every fall.

So, while it is possible to breed a five-day cow, it won't be easy. These genetic aberrations only occur sporadically, so we must always be on the look out for them. Look for signs of one cow being drowsier than the others, especially on the weekends. Keep an eye on any cows that seem to be cranky and give less milk on Sundays. Although it may take several generations of careful breeding to develop a true five-day cow, it will be worth it.

Just think, our ancestors only option for a five-day cow was to literally "put a cork in it" while for us it's only a matter of time.

# FIRST CALF HEIFERS

First calf heifers are a devil to milk. Take 717, for example. She was the most difficult heifer to milk that I have ever encountered, a seven on the Richter scale, if you catch my drift.

I should have realized that she was BIG trouble the first time I locked her in the milking parlor. As I approached her she had that same look of panic I get whenever my wife invites me to accompany her to a hooked rug exhibit. This heifer was willing to try anything to get out of there.

Her first kick was a real prizewinner! Not only was it high and outside, but it also had force, conviction, and, above all, tremendous speed. When I came to, the side of my head was bleeding and my glasses were laying on the parlor floor, minus one lens.

What a sinking feeling I had as I searched for the missing bifocal lens amidst the dense muck. Luckily, I spotted it resting almost under the rear foot of the next cow in line. Retrieving it carefully took nerves of steel as another kick was eminent. Apparently the kick's force was enough to both bend my glasses frame and cut my face. I gingerly snapped the lens into place and straightened the frame enough so that it almost fit, and then reached for the anti-kick device that I should have used from the start.

She's still not speaking to me, but she does tolerate being milked better than I expected. Soon she will be a cow and accept the parlor routine gracefully. And I will never be over-confident around a first calf heifer again, at least not until the next one freshens!

# REAR FEET FIRST

Have you ever watched a cow get up? If you haven't, you really should. It's more fun than going to the circus. Since most cows weigh more than thirteen hundred pounds, getting that much weight from a lying position to a standing position is no easy feat.

The first thing a cow must do when she decides to stand up is to raise her rear end and get both rear feet planted squarely under her. Since simply doing this would require a tremendous amount of brute strength, a cow, as dumb as you might think she is, uses an important scientific principle to help her: momentum. That's right, in order to raise her hind end, she must first throw all of her weight forward in a tremendous lunge, powerful enough to smash a two-by-six board. She must have space enough to lunge forward or she literally cannot get up. With her back legs now standing, she merely finishes the job by standing up with her front legs.

Sounds easy, doesn't it? A cow has to get up that way, rear feet first. She simply cannot get up if she raises up on her front feet first. This happens occasionally when a cow forgets how to get up. She will sit there, like a frog on a lily pad, looking all around and wondering how she got into this position. Quite often it takes a great deal of salesmanship to convince her that the only way she will ever get to a standing position is to first lie back down and get up, rear end first. Once standing, particularly if she has been lying down for some time, she has to go to the bathroom. Cows have never learned to, as we say, "hold it."

So the next time you are too busy to go to the circus or you think cows are dumb animals, just watch them perform the complicated task of getting up.

# Chapter 3

## LIVING ON A BACK ROAD

Our farm is on a back road. In my youth it was really a back road. Since we were the single year-round home on the road at the time, the road was maintained only as far as our driveway. The remaining mile was simply two wheel tracks with grass growing between them, shaded by tall trees on either side.

Unfortunately, progress set in and now the road is wide and paved and proudly sports landscaped shoulders. This once scenic, little-used path has turned into everyone's short cut. From morning till night hundreds of vehicles whiz past our driveway. The parade starts early in the morning with developers' pickups, followed by neighbors on their way to work. During the day we are entertained by a constant flow of sundry farm machinery, farmers in pickups, and realtors in Lincolns. Later there will be school buses and our neighbors returning tired from work, and an occasional pretty girl on a bike, but I digress.

One advantage of living on a back road is missing the steady stream of salesmen that those on the main road seem to attract. Even so, the truck loaded with steel gates, the aerial photographer, and the roof painters from Georgia still manage to find me, as do a bevy of hunters.

The only time that I regret living off the beaten path is when I must give a stranger directions to the farm. After describing obscure landmarks and unsigned intersections, I wish I could say, "Just go east on the state road for seven miles and you can't miss us."

Please don't think that we are lonely, though. Our driveway is graced with milk inspectors, our daughter's suitors, hunters in the fall, and lost people asking for directions in the spring. How lucky I am to be able to work at home and still see the world pass right by my doorstep. Yes, I miss the old back road, but the new road is much more exciting.

# WHAT'S IN A NAME?

In the good old days, when farms were smaller, individual fields were referred to by convenient, understandable names that were recognizable to all who worked on the farm. Now, with computerized crop, fertilizer and weed control records on many more fields, beautiful old names like "deer haven" and "woodchuck city" have fallen prey to cold, sterile combinations of numbers and letters.

I long for the days of old when, with a mere reference to the blacksmith's shop field, everyone immediately knew what you were talking about, even though the blacksmith shop had been gone for nearly one hundred years. Sometimes a field was named for its shape, such as the "fish" field. Since this field was prone to frequent flooding, I always thought that there were fish left in the corn rows after the water receded, giving the field its name!

A road divides our farm with all the land on the west side of the road referred to as the "west lot." When I was a kid this was a huge area, with a hill great for sleigh riding. ample pasture with a pond, and large fields of alfalfa and corn. When I grew up I was amazed to find that the west lot was only 30 acres of land, better suited to wildlife and Christmas trees than agriculture. Where all that beautiful land went I'll never know!

Sometimes the topography of a field clearly explains its name. One farm has a high hill with a steep drop off. Picture yourself standing on this hill on a windy day and you will understand why this was dubbed the "hang gliding field." Sometimes the name denotes something that happened in that field, whether it was a particularly bad tractor sinking or maybe an embarrassing situation having to do with a lack of clothing on a hot day and a surprise visitor.

Most often a field's name refers to something that's not there any more. Any lime truck driver will tell you that the orchard field and the lime kiln field will have neither in them. And don't be surprised if you find some strange stones in the graveyard field.

Numbering and lettering fields may be necessary to make sure there are no mistakes by all those involved in caring for our land, but field 101 will always be the chestnut tree field to me.

# LIFE ON A HILL

We live on a hill. I always thought this gave us many advantages over those poor souls who don't. For one thing, we never have to worry about floods. For another, starting a tractor with a dead battery is easy: roll it off, pop the clutch and away you go.

But there are times when living on a hill is not an advantage because things can roll when they are not supposed to. That's what happened to us one June. A loaded silage wagon began to roll, all by itself, downhill toward the swimming pool. Don't get ahead of me now.

No words can describe the helpless feeling of watching a loaded wagon box, with no sense of direction, gain speed, its tongue bouncing along searching for something to crush.

Of course, it could have been worse. It could have hit the old empty concrete stave silo, which certainly would have caused it to buckle and tumble into a million pieces. It could have gone through the rickety split rail fence and into the swimming pool, or, worse yet, it could have hit the pool house and pushed it into the pool.

You have to realize this all happened before our very eyes in less time than it takes to sneeze. Yes, I thought about grabbing the tongue and pulling it uphill, but not for long. I've tripped over my own feet enough times in less perilous situations to know I didn't have a chance. So, I stepped aside and watched the inevitable happen. In its path were three cars. Two were old, depreciated, well-worn small cars that had served us well but were of little real value. The third was my wife's late model luxury car, the only car we have ever owned with functioning air conditioning and a built-in four speaker stereo which was the envy of hearing impaired teenagers everywhere. We loved that car. It was quiet, comfortable and effortless to drive. Needless to say, that's the one the runaway wagon chose to hit.

It hit with a loud "wump" sound the other two cars will not soon forget. Who says nothing exciting ever happens on the farm?

# MORE ACRES

I am not one to gloat, but I feel my farm has a distinct advantage over those in valleys with their large flat fields. I know, valley farmers think they have the best farms available, with deep fertile soils, plenty of moisture and open areas large enough to make wide machinery practical. I, however, have something they will never have - hills. That's my secret weapon, my key to high productivity, that ultimate unspoken advantage which separates me from those envious flat-landers.

It is usually at this point that someone asks, "Why does having hills make your farm better than anyone else's?" The answer is simple. I have more land. That's right, looking straight down on my farm, the way an aerial photographer does, it looks like any other farm, with large open fields. But I know, with my rolling steep cropland, that I get more acres of the earth's surface than my slope-challenged neighbors do. Some fields are so steep and so rolling that I'm sure to gain an acre or more in those fields.

This concept can be easily illustrated by taking a sheet of paper and looking down on it while leaning over it. Now take that same sheet of paper and push each end toward the center. You will see a rolling action than turns a flat piece of paper into one with high hills and low valleys. At the same time you will notice that the paper now covers less area than it did while lying flat. It is easy to see that the space lost on each end is equal to the surface gained on the steep hillsides.

This provides irrefutable proof that I am working more land per acre than my incline-deprived neighbors. This personal bonanza allows me to grow more total feed for my cows from less land, the goal of humanitarians everywhere.

I won't bore you any more with other wonderful attributes of hilly land. Do me one favor, though. Please don't mention this to my assessor. Next time - the advantage of rocks.

# BLESSED ROCKS

For those blessed with a rock-strewn farm, I have good news. While you have been cursing the day you decided to farm between the rocks instead of seeking a farm free of God's little bonuses, I have been researching the many advantages of rocks.

It turns out that rocks have gotten a bad rap because of rumors started by envious river-bottom farmers. To begin with, rocks actually do warm the soil in the spring. That's why you always see weeds growing out of cracks in sidewalks in March. In wet years, rocks provide a base to keep you from sinking into the mud. Rocks also keep you from going too fast in the field or from mowing too close to the ground.

In reality there are three kinds of rocks: pickers, sliders and painters. Pickers are small enough to pick up and put in a tractor bucket or onto a stone boat. Sliders are too big to pick up; you must slide them up a plank to get them onto a stone boat. Painters are too large to lift, slide or dig up. If they stick up very much they are painted neon orange so farm machinery can dodge them. Those close to the road can be painted decoratively.

Rocks are also great for walls, planters and paperweights. Once thought a burden, picking rocks provides wonderful opportunities for families to spend time together. A family that picks together sticks together!

Studies reveal that picking rock is one of the best exercises for toning tummy muscles and abs that those magazines in supermarket racks keep promoting.

Picking rock can also measure the seriousness of salesmen. Any salesman who will put down an order pad and help pick rock demonstrates a real understanding of how to gain a prospect's trust and ultimate sale.

When I was young I asked my mother how the boulders in a neighbor's farm got there. She responded, "The devil was flying over with his apron full of rocks and at that exact spot his apron strings broke." I always doubted the validity of this story, but never had nerve enough to shatter my mother's faith in the devil.

Whatever the reason, some of us are blessed with rock-strewn farms. If you ever need any rocks, I am only a stone's throw away.

# HAND SIGNALS

One of the most difficult problems facing farmers today is finding a way to communicate over the roar of the tractor engine or whine of a smoke alarm.  At last the problem is solved for I have devised a complete set of simple, easy-to-learn hand signals that will make any message clear and understandable, regardless of the background noise.

These signals are divided into two groups.  The one-handed signals are to be used when the tractor is moving; the two-handed ones are only used when the tractor is safely stopped and the brakes are on.

In order to keep the total number of hand signals to a minimum, each one has several meanings.  This not only saves time but also adds a little fun to an otherwise stressful exchange.  For example, holding up your hand and making the numeral one with your index finger may mean one more load before lunch, please bring me a drink of water next trip, or may I go to the bathroom now?  You get the idea, right?  You can even devise your own hand signals on the spot, for any situation.

One that we use frequently is done by holding one's head in one's hands and rocking back and forth.  This would signify, "The darned thing broke again." Or it might mean "I'm tired and I want to go to bed," or it could mean, "Oh no, she's backing right over the battery charger, again."

It's so easy and so much fun that it's amazing that no one ever thought of this communication system before.

# GIVING DIRECTIONS

Farmers spend far too much time giving directions. Why? Because the people doing the asking weren't given proper directions in the first place. Either that or they are the type who would get lost racing the Indianapolis 500. Fortunately, farmers are usually good-natured about helping lost motorists, but they should be forgiven for having some fun at the same time. Just because I am on my back underneath a truck why do so many people think that I am not busy?

When I give directions I strive to make them brief, concise and as confusing as possible. One thing that I like to tell people is to watch for the blue house with the white mailbox on the corner, when either there is no house at all on that corner, or the house is white and the mailbox is blue. Another pet trick is to give misleading mileage estimates. There is nothing more disconcerting to a lost soul than going exactly 4.3 miles, only to find that their destination is still ten miles down the road.

My all-time favorite is to send someone in such a way that they end up back at my farm. When they get upset, I tell them that that was just a test to see if they can follow directions, before I waste my valuable time telling them how to get to where they wanted to go in the first place.

Another way to make giving directions light-hearted is to use colorful descriptions of landmarks like "Turn right where the schoolhouse used to be," or "It's the left just before the old Schultz place." Often I act upset at not being able to remember if the turn is the second or third left past the first or second bridge, so I carry on a conversation with myself about the changes that have taken place since I last took that route.

Be sure to include enough useless details to make remembering the key decisions difficult. I am sure if you follow these tips you will find yourself spending far less time giving directions a second time to lost motorists and more time napping under the truck.

# THE EASY WAY

Everyone likes the easy way. As an old adage says, "If you want the easy way, ask a lazy man." That applies to people, other animals, and especially to cows.

Ours is a modern, efficient dairy farm. We start our calves in hutches, then move them to tiny free stalls so they can become cubiclely-oriented. As they grow they are moved into appropriately larger free stalls until they graduate to the big barn and become cows. All the while they are fed a complete ration from the ubiquitous mixer wagon. With all they want to eat and drink and a clean, dry place to lie down, they certainly have found the "easy way."

So now let me tell you about an eye-opening experience we had this summer. We used to pasture all of our animals each summer, as most small farms did. Over the years we cleared and gradually converted our old pastureland into productive farmland and went to feeding our cattle from horizontal storages, eliminating pasturing entirely.

The result was higher production per cow, more cows per acre and more work for us, as we were doing the harvesting, not the cows. We still had three acres of land too steep and wet to crop, but near the house, so we had the bright idea of fencing it in and letting a few dry cows eat the lush grass and bask in the sun while they were on vacation.

Sounds like a Club Med for cows to me, but not to them. They were not happy campers at all. They were not used to harvesting their own food, walking more than a few feet for water or experiencing the unfamiliar feeling of soil under their feet. I don't think they ever adjusted to or appreciated the wonderful opportunity granted to them. When the time came to return to life on concrete floors and full feed bunks, they literally ran all the way into the barn.

Does this mean that modern cows are no longer able to sustain themselves on pasture once they have enjoyed the "easy life?" Of course not. Cows, like people will do what they must to survive. But given a choice, when hungry, people choose the drive-thru and cows head for the feed bunk.

# FENCES

Fences are kind of like marriages, easy to build but difficult to maintain. When we used to fence the entire farm, I grew to hate building and repairing wire fences. Barbed wire would cut my hands and woven wire fences were expensive and a major project to build.

Boy, was I tickled pink when we found that the animals grew and produced better in a well-bedded and well-ventilated barn than when they were out pacing the fence lines, searching for that missing staple or broken wire so they could finally find out if the grass really was greener on the other side of the fence.

Pasturing is still the best use of odd pieces of land too steep, rocky, or wet to till, but, fortunately we have very little of that. We prefer the risk of getting stuck in those marginal fields or tipping over in them, rather than resorting to building a fence around them.

I'm talking about permanent fences here, not the temporary kind popular in a rotational grazing program. Too often my permanent fences turned out to be temporary ones, like the time the snow got so deep and hard that the heifers could walk on the snow, right over the top of my beautiful three strand barbed wire fence. Maybe they thought the snow was whiter on the other side!

I never had much luck with electric fences. It seemed like the only time the power was on was when I tried to slide under it with too short a shirttail. I didn't know I could run so fast.

I learned fence building from my father. He always stressed the importance of using locust posts because they would last longer than any other wood. The old timers used to say, "A locust post would last two years longer than a rock." A dry locust post was almost as hard as a rock! Short staples might go in far enough to hold wire tight to the post, but no hammer was heavy enough to drive a long staple into a dry locust post.

Fences and marriages, in order to survive years of stretching, storms, and sunshine, require strong posts, frequent attention, and occasional tightening.

# PHONE FANTASIES

I have always been annoyed at the flagrant pretentiousness of cell phone users. First it was car phones. Their owners were usually well-dressed young people, chatting away on their car phone, while driving the latest, popular, hard-to-find foreign car with a bashed in front corner. They might just as well have worn a sign in big letters on each side of the car, saying, "I can afford a car phone but I still can't drive."

Then small portable phones became more reliable and affordable. Now it is not uncommon to stumble onto a beleaguered husband in the far corner of Wal-Mart saying into his flip phone, "Where are you, Martha? You said you would meet me in sporting goods two hours ago and you are no where to be seen."

Actually, that was the way I used to feel. You see, now I have one. In fact, there are four cell phones in the family, all interconnected, so they can be used as wireless intercoms or as conventional phones. No longer are they playthings of the rich and famous. Now they are essential communication tools, irreplaceable in the successful operation of a busy family farm. So much so, in fact, that I'm reluctant to shut mine off in a movie, meeting, or dentist chair.

It is amazing how my attitude on cell phones has changed. Now I can call David or Pat anytime from where ever I am. The bad news is that they can call me at anytime, too. It will be hard to explain how I am just finishing the back 40 when she hears in the background, "You want fries with that?" Now I can order pizza from the tractor and meet the deliveryman on the way back from spreading manure.

With cabs on tractors now there is also the possibility of making a lot of calls while doing boring jobs like mowing or disking. Trying to make complicated decisions while planting may lead to seeing an aerial photo of your cornfield in a magazine labeled, "New corn maze proves popular."

There are over 80 million cell phones in use now, with more being sold everyday to those who believe the headline, "The phone is free if you buy from us."

It won't be long before we will no longer talk to each other. We will all be busy answering our cell phones.

# KEEPING THINGS ROLLING

Did you ever notice how dependent we are on simple things like rubber tires? Between the forage harvester, dump wagon, two tractors and a forage wagon, we must keep 20 tires functioning just to harvest haylage, plus 14 more tires to mow and rake the crop. It's deflating to realize that 16 tires are needed just to clean the barns and spread the manure daily. Beads of sweat began to form on my brow as I realized it takes six tires to plant corn, ten tires just to feed the cows, and 14 tires to plow and disk. There are over 100 tires on all the vehicles and implements on this farm, all of which need to be kept inflated and in good condition. It makes me tired just thinking about it.

When I complained to my daughter that the rear tire on the big tractor went flat the day the tire repairman went on vacation, she laughed and said, "That sounds like the title of a country western song." I didn't get any sympathy from her.

Considering the number of nails, stones and pieces of steel laying around the farm, just begging to be run over, everyday without a flat on something is a joy to behold.

It seems like we are always under pressure to get most of the work done in the least amount of time, so taking that extra step to check all the tires on our implements seems like a waste of valuable time.

Usually a quick glance to see if one corner of a tractor or spreader is sagging is all the precaution that is taken. The old adage, ""There is never time to do it right the first time, but always time to do it over," certainly applies here. Just walking once around a machine, observing tires, wheel nuts, and any loose bolts, doesn't take long and could prevent an ecological disaster later.

Now that I have put the whole tire subject in perspective, I'll try not to be too upset when I find the next flat tire. After all, one out of a hundred is not bad.

# AUTOMATIC SHIFT

I must be a good listener. I recently endured a long tale of woe from one of my yuppie friends on how difficult it was to find an upscale automobile with standard shift. It must be anyone with an "automatic" might be seen as a wimp, worm, or weakling. I know that shifting a five speed soon becomes automatic, but I challenge anyone to gracefully pull into heavy traffic on a main road with an ice cream cone in one hand and the steering wheel and shift lever in the other.

To me, a car with automatic transmission is my reward for the hours spent shifting all the tractors and trucks on the farm. For example, twice a day we scrape our free stall barn with a back blade on a small standard shift tractor. In doing this seemingly minor chore, each year I shift approximately 7,284 times and travel over 150 miles, all without ever leaving the barn!

And then there are those silage trucks, all with five speeds and two speed axles. What a lot of fun they are. You spend so much time either shifting up or shifting down or split shifting, it's a wonder you don't forget where you are going. "What is split shifting?" you ask.

It is the art of simultaneously shifting the transmission up and down at the same time. Detailed instructions on how to do this are usually printed on the ceiling of the truck cab. I would caution you, however, not to wait until you are in the middle of a steep hill, loaded and losing momentum, to read the directions in detail. With diligent practice anyone can split shift a two speed axle flawlessly most of the time. Missing a split shift, however, can leave you petrified, paralyzed, and positively powerless.

A loaded silage truck is not so much a vehicle as it is a guided missile. One fully loaded with bombs, oops, I mean silage, weighs more than a small house. Picture a small cottage going down hill faster than a heifer in horn fly season with about as much stopping capacity, bearing down on a Volvo station wagon full of kids, and you will appreciate why having a car shift for itself is such a luxury.

Give me a rocky road ice cream cone and an automatic shift anytime.

# CORN PLANTING

The wet spring of 1996 will be remembered almost as long as the dry summer of '95. When the rain finally stopped for a few days, our precision corn planting team sprang into action. Our fleet of 30 year-old John Deere 4020's begrudgingly met the challenge of planting half our corn acreage in one beautiful, sun-drenched weekend. It was a sight to behold - their faded green paint stood in stark contrast to the fertile brown soil. My son, David, skillfully plowed, my wife gamely followed with the disk harrow, and finally I came scurrying along with the planter, vainly trying to keep up. By Sunday night all the fields within sight of the house were all prepared and anxiously awaited their annual visit from the great corn planter.

I started the last field as dusk slowly crept across the landscape. And, for the next four bone-chilling hours I planted an entire huge field, roughly the size of eight mall parking lots, in the pitch dark. Well, not entirely dark, the tractor did have lights, of sorts. At least it provided enough light to see the planter behind and barely enough to avoid hedgerows, hogshead-sized rocks, and haystacks. It was a good thing I knew the field, I thought, having planted it in daylight several times. Otherwise, as the corn came up, the field would look like a garden maze with no entrances or exits. It was fun pounding away in the dark with the old tractor and planter; I was one with the soil and the night. The field seemed to melt away until finally the last rows were planted. It was one a.m., but I had triumphed over

Mother Nature and the weatherman. What a great feeling of victory that was! It felt so good, I couldn't wait to get started planting again on Monday.

Then it happened. While servicing the planter the following day, David noticed that something was missing. It seems that all the little things that keep the seed from going too deep were gone. So was one of the gauge wheels. Not only that, but one of the row markers was almost ripped off the machine.

Yes, my riding away merrily in the dark surely took its toll on the old planter. How was I to know anything was wrong? The electronic monitor told me seeds were being dropped methodically; occasional glances assured me that the planter was still behind me. The constant din let me know that all the chains and sprockets were turning. How many other details could I be expected to keep an eye upon? So what, if some of the corn was planted so deep it may take weeks for it to finally break from the ground into the morning sunlight. It will get there; it always has. So what if one row marker is broken. Who needs straight rows anyway? After all, everyone knows that crooked rows produce more corn.

One thing is for sure though, David is not going to let me plant any more corn in the dark again this year.

# TALKING THERMOMETERS

One of the most difficult skills an animal husbandman must master is reading a glass oral thermometer. I would have said "rectal" thermometer, but this is a family column. Besides, taking a cow's temperature orally would be almost as hard as getting her to put on a pair of leotards. That's why I was delighted to find an amazing electronic talking thermometer in our local drugstore. And what's more, it was on sale - my prayers had been answered. I snatched one from the display and ran for the checkout. Obviously, it was not selling well because not everyone had as much trouble as I did trying to find that elusive mercury column.

The good news is that the thermometer works beautifully. Simply put it where the directions tell you to, wait until the temperature stabilizes, and a pleasant female voice will say, "Your body temperature is 101.5 degrees" or whatever the cow's temperature is. So far I haven't gotten it to say anything else, but I keep hoping.

So enthused with this amazing electronic gadget am I that I look forward to the development of other devices with soothing voices to further simplify a farmer's life. At the top of my wish list is a talking stethoscope that will tell me everything I ever wanted to know about a sick cow. Everything from heart rate to rumen function would be explained by a voice that could even prescribe remedies or medications for that particular problem.

Sound good? Let's not stop there. The computer chip has the potential for making our lives even more peaceful and productive. For example, wouldn't it be nice to have a device that could tell when a cow is going to calve, whether the vet is going to get there in time, or if your wife is still mad at you?

Also needed is a device to tell when the haylage is dry enough, when the chopper will breakdown, and when dinner will be ready. I don't know how I ever managed without a synthesized voice telling me what to do. Since I am like most farmers, too busy to read the directions, I certainly hope that all these gadgets come with a talking manual.

# MY BALER

Did you ever notice that farm machines sometimes have a mind of their own? Take my baler for example. The kicker keeps playing tricks on me. It will work fine just long enough to convince me that it is infallible. Then, when I least expect it, it will malfunction, pushing bales under the throwing pan, making them as easy to extract as pulling an oversize calf from a young heifer.

Next it will perform perfectly just long enough to build my confidence and then "bang". There it goes again, trying to tell me that it much prefers the cool, dry tool shed to the hot and dusty hay field, given the thankless job of throwing an endless supply of heavy, scratchy bales into an unfeeling, unappreciative wagon.

It works best when I've called the repairman to see if he can find the trouble. Then it works flawlessly, throwing bale after bale into the wagon with a steady rhythm, making me look like a fool. Someday I am going to get even. I am going to call the repairman without telling the baler. I can play this game, too!

# TRACTOR MEALS

Because of a worldwide shortage of time and the constant urge from Cooperative Extension for farmers to become more efficient, I am proposing one way to gain at least one hour of work time each and every day.

That's right, at least one hour each day is wasted and all productive work is halted just to eat lunch. That's an hour that could be put to good use by combining lunch with necessary tractor work. Why not? You are already sitting down anyway.

The challenge is to find foods that can be easily unwrapped, prepared, enjoyed, and cleaned up after, while manipulating steering wheels, hydraulic levers, and throttle controls. Anything sticky like barbecued chicken, candied apples, or popsicles must be avoided. They just make the steering wheel tacky, adding new meaning to the phrase, "Tearing yourself away."

Likewise, foods that are awkward to eat like corn on the cob, barbecued spare ribs, and tacos, won't be much fun either. As you can see, the list of acceptable foods is readily dwindling. For example, an orange might seem to be a harmless and nourishing snack, but the last time I tried peeling one while planting corn the rows behind me looked like ocean waves. Then I tried watermelon. Big mistake. It was good but the ping of the seeds hitting the windshield drove me crazy.

That leaves the sandwich, a favorite of farmers since bread was invented. But not just any sandwich. The filling has to be cohesive enough so that its contents won't dribble out all over your lap, solid enough to keep from getting your fingers sticky, and dry enough so as not to soak through the bread. That's why egg salad and spaghetti have little sandwich potential, while cold cuts and peanut butter with jelly do.

Finding something acceptable for dessert is even harder. Anything requiring two hands like jello or a hot fudge sundae is out. So is anything requiring a microwave like s'mores or hot apple pie. That leaves us with a food that requires no preparation, can be served cold, and will fit in your pocket - an apple.

Choosing a beverage is relatively simple: it must be cold, in individual containers easily opened and closed with one hand, spill-proof, and fit any size cup holder.

So you see, not only is eating lunch on the tractor a great time saver, it can also be an exciting adventure and much more fun than eating warmed over tuna casserole at the kitchen table.

# Chapter 4

## UNDERSTANDING BOVINE BEHAVIOR

Have you ever wondered how a newborn calf knows which end of a cow to suck? Or how a cow knows that if she licks a gate latch long enough she will eventually get it open? A cow does many things that seem to come naturally to her, yet are behaviors that almost seem self-taught. Like kicking the dip cup out of your hand at the most inopportune moment, or using her tongue for a handkerchief.

There can be only one explanation for this phenomenon. Just like every new computer comes with Windows on it, cows also come preprogrammed. The only differences are that a cow's program cannot be updated as easily and learning its operation requires more patience.

That's why cows don't think about it, they just do it. Their innate programming lifts the burden of thinking from their shoulders, or heads, freeing them to do things like swishing at flies with their tails, scratching behind their ears with their rear feet or simultaneously coughing and defecating, usually all over your clean boots, without ever considering why they are doing it or what effect their actions have on others.

In retrospect, we are very fortunate that cows do come already programmed. It would be almost impossible to teach a cow to chew her cud or lick off a newborn calf, given her almost non-existent mental capacity.

Cows accept new ways of doing things about as well as a man who has been married for 40 years. They may accept it, but they won't be happy about it.

The good thing about cows being preprogrammed is that they never need to be saved on a disk, rebooted, updated, downloaded, revised or reformatted.

# DO COWS HAVE FEELINGS?

I know I have been spending entirely too much time with the cows when I start treating them just like people. In many ways, cows are like people. They each have a distinct personality and experience many of the same emotions as people do.

A cow is certainly capable of feeling such common emotions as love, hate, fear and happiness. After all, her love for her newborn calf is legendary; her hatred of pills is understandable; her fear of veterinarians is undeniable and her happiness over fresh feed is a joy to behold. It's feelings of anger, compassion and guilt that I'm not sure of.

Do cows get angry? I don't think so. Disappointed, yes; ticked off, yes; but I don't think that cows are capable of being angry or carrying a grudge. How about compassion? I doubt it. As much as I like and understand cows, they are not, by their very nature, the compassionate, patient, understanding animals that everyone thinks they are. In fact, I'll let you in on a nasty little secret: A cow is only interested in one thing, and that's her own survival. If you detect anything that looks like compassion, she's just putting on a show in hopes of getting some extra feed.

Now guilt is another question entirely. I am of the opinion that no matter how bad a mess a cow gets herself into, she is not capable of feeling guilty about it.

Disappointment is a better word. That look in her eyes says it all. "Why didn't I steal more grain when I had the chance," or "A few more minutes and I could have destroyed all the tomato plants, too." No, cows never feel guilty.

What they do feel mostly, though, is hunger and thirst. That's probably why I think cows are like people.

# COWS ARE LIKE PEOPLE

After a lifetime of working with and for cows, I have come to the conclusion that cows are just like people. "How are they similar, other than being large, aimless animals with a huge appetite?" you might ask.

To begin with, cows each have definite individual and clearly recognizable personalities. Just like humans, cows never do anything unless and until they absolutely have to. Cows never plan ahead.

They have an insatiable appetite and childlike curiosity. In many ways, cows are like politicians. When something good happens they are the first ones on the scene, but when something bad happens they act very, very meek and innocent. There is nothing funnier than discovering a cow where she shouldn't be. Cows will be standing knee deep in broken bales and spilled grain with the most wide-eyed, innocent, "Who me?" look on their faces, not unlike a five year old child caught with his hand in the cookie jar. Since the average age in my herd is five years, I guess that is to be expected.

Cows are not inherently neat. Like many men, cows appreciate a clean place to eat and sleep, but depend on others to pick up after them. Also, like men, cows don't ask for directions. Fortunately, they don't have to travel far! Like some people with short attention spans, cows don't need much to entertain them. Any kind of movement can pique their interest. Anything from a prowling cat to a windblown paper bag can keep cows occupied for as long as three minutes at a time.

There are still more ways that cows seem like people. Cows find it difficult to show appreciation for anything you do for them. They act confused much of the time. It is hard for cows to communicate their true feelings to those they know best, unless you consider staring, licking and kicking as signs of affection. Yes, cows are like humans in many ways. But let us never forget that with proper care and feeding, the dairy cow can be a very productive, exasperating and lovable animal.

# SHORT-LIVED MOTHERLY CONCERN

The newborn calf was hard to feed. Not the ordinary slow-drinking, apathetic, six swallows and take a breath type, she had her own way of taking forever. Her biggest problem was the placement of her tongue, which seemed to slip out of the side of her mouth, rather than stay securely under the rubber nipple of the plastic calf feeding bottle, a feat which all good calves innately know how to do.

So, resigning myself to a long siege, I turned a plastic five gallon pail upside down in her four by four pen adjacent to the free stall area and sat down to make myself more comfortable. I cradled the calf's head on one arm and the bottle on the other. She was trying to suck but her side-saddle tongue resulted in a great loss of sucking efficiency.

While this little drama was unfolding, I noticed that the calf's mother was standing just over the wall from us, watching with the scornful eye of a mother who knows that she could do a better job than any human being. I am just thankful that her motherly concern was not punctuated with frequent loud and agonizing cries.

This poignant scene reminded me of my father's keen observation of a fresh cow's heart-rending concern for her calf. He once said, "It almost breaks your heart to separate a fresh cow from her new born calf because she will show the most tearful anxiety over her loss that you could ever imagine by pacing back and forth and bawling continuously.  She usually keeps this up for about three days and then forgets all about her new calf, until she has another one, of course."

# HABITS

A habit is a wonderful thing. Once established, it can be depended upon to free your mind from making many stressful decisions each day. If it were not for our ability to form habits, we would spend hours trying to decide when to get up, what to have for breakfast, and whether to get dressed or not. One good habit is to always put things back where they belong. That way you will always be able to find them.

Bad habits, on the other hand, can be terrible things. Bad habits can cause you pain, loss of sleep, and brief moments of ecstasy. The secret of success is to work at developing good habits and breaking the bad ones. After all, habits are like being married; all the important decisions are made for you.

Cows depend on habits for their very existence. Actually doing the same thing at the same time every day is about all they can handle. Oddly, we think we have trained them, when the truth is, it is they who have trained us. They know they will be fed and milked at the same time everyday. All they have to do is be in the right place at the right time.

Bad habits are much easier to form than good ones. That's because they are devious and sly. They sneak up on you when you least expect it and bam, there you are eating a jelly donut when all you were going to do was look in the bakery window. Or maybe someone stops by on a very busy day and, without warning, you find you have wasted an hour discussing everything from milk pricing to skirt lengths. Beware, bad habits make a habit of taking you by surprise.

The good news is, once a habit is formed, you will find it very hard to break.

# COWS ARE CURIOUS

Cows are curious creatures. How do they satisfy that curiosity? For them, it's not easy. We humans, when coming across a strange object, can indulge our curious nature in a plethora of ways. We can feel it, pick at it, fondle it, rotate it and thoroughly inspect it. It is easy for us because we have hands to feel and pinch things. Cows, on the other hand, have very few ways to quench their insatiable curiosities.

Their primary investigative tool is their huge, wet, clammy, wide-nostrilled nose. That's right, a cow will always sniff of something strange immediately after deciding that the object is inanimate and will not jump up and bite her.

I often wonder how much cows really learn by this indiscriminate sniffing. A cow really doesn't smell that good. We all know that, but what I mean is a cow's sense of smell is not that keen. Sure, they know the difference between silage and cow dung, and who doesn't? If a cow's sense of smell were as sensitive as they would lead you to believe, cows would be used to track escaped criminals. Every sheriff's department would have a bovine unit for sniffing out hidden drugs, and old suspense movies would all have a scene showing two jail escapees hiding in a snake infested swamp, being startled by a distant "moo." They would cringe muttering, "We're done for now, Max, they've called out the cows."

Because they can't smell much, cows rely mostly on their last line of defense, the "tongue." Cows lick things to see if they are edible or drinkable, but mostly just to knock them over. At this point it is only fair to warn you, as pretty and affectionate as a cow's tongue appears, before touching it, remember, this tongue is the only tool a cow has. Its coarse sandpaper-like surface probably has been used to lick a salt block, clean a newborn calf and to lick herself in some very hard to reach places, if you catch my drift. A cow's tongue is better seen than felt.

Curiosity may have killed the cat and it quite often gets cows in trouble, too.

# BEWILDERED

As I closed the parlor gate in front of her, a look of bewilderment swept over the cow's face.  I could almost hear her saying, "What did he do that for?" and "Now what do I do?" and finally, "Uh-oh, I must be in real trouble now!"

It occurred to me that a cow's life must be one bewildering event after another.  While we may envy a cow's simple, repetitive, and utterly predictable existence, we fail to realize how many difficult decisions she faces daily.  Considering that the average age of a dairy cow is just over five years, I guess that their decision-making skills haven't fully matured.  That must be why they never go in the direction you point them, but then, five year old children don't either.

Actually cows will do almost anything as long as you do it the same time every day.  For example, when I started farming, the old stable needed to be remodeled, which meant paving part of the barnyard.  To do this the whole herd temporarily had to enter the barn through a door with a two foot high step.  The first day was a problem getting them to hop up into the barn, but after several days they all acted like Olympic high jump stars, taking this obstacle in stride with nary a "moo" of complaint.

Maybe cows aren't as stupid as we think they are.  Maybe they aren't as bewildered as they appear.  Perhaps it is all an act to gain our sympathy.  Is it their clever minds working overtime?  No, they really are that confused, astonished, and perplexed at each little disruption in their lives. But that's all right. To a cow, being bewildered is a way of life.

# THE COWS ARE PLOTTING AGAINST ME!

When I entered the barn that morning the cows all looked so innocent, quietly chewing their cuds and playing their favorite game of "staring at the wall," while in reality, they had been up all night devising a treacherous plan. But, unbeknownst to them, I had overheard their ringleader, #548, say, "He thinks he is so smart, just wait."

With a gleam in her eye and a quick glance over her shoulder she said, "Here's the plan. We'll all go into the parlor nicely so he won't suspect a thing. Then, when I give the signal, we will all lie down at once right on top of those darn clucking milking machines. He'll be so upset that he will call in all the experts - the vet, the county agent, even the power company, thinking stray voltage was the cause."

"Then, when all those so-called experts arrive we will all just stand there chewing our cuds as if nothing had happened."

With a mischievous grin, #548 continued, "He will look like a fool. Nobody will blame us, poor, innocent, dumb animals, and we will have something to chuckle about all winter."

Although it sounded like a good strategy to them, little did they know that I had my own little plan, too. I am going to turn off the computer feeder for 24 hours. They will be so upset that I hope they will forget all about their devious little scheme.

# A SECOND JOB FOR COWS

I have noticed that my cows are wasting entirely too much time. Granted, the time spent in the holding area, being milked and eating at the feed bunk are absolutely necessary. However, they seem to be spending an inordinate amount of time just lying in their free stalls, chewing their cuds, or staring blankly into space. There must be something that they can be doing to bring in some extra income so I can finally afford a tractor with an air-conditioned cab, just like God intended.

Admittedly, I have not discussed this proposal with the cows as yet, but I am considering several possibilities. From the ads placed in the back pages of seedy magazines there seems to be a shortage of people capable of stuffing envelopes. Cows should be especially good at this, particularly at licking the envelopes as well as the stamps.

Although teaching them to reupholster furniture is also a possibility, I am afraid that their innate carelessness would make tool loss a monumental problem, not to mention the difficultly of holding and hitting those little brass tacks.

Knitting ski caps is also being explored. If that doesn't work out, there is always a great demand in the VCR repair field. The possibilities are endless. I wonder if this is the "alternatives in agriculture" everyone is talking about.

## COWS ARE EASILY SATISFIED

I like working with cows because they are so easily satisfied. All they need to be happy is ample feed, water, a dry place to lie down and their cuds. There is no whining and complaining about working conditions, temperature, or lack of variety in their selection of food. Maybe it's their inability to know how badly off they really are or, worse yet, how much better off they could be.

Cows are happiest when they are not faced with a lot of decisions. To us, being housed all winter in an unheated building with exactly the same food day after day might be hard to take, but to a cow that's bliss. She knows that every morning and evening when she exits the milking parlor there will be fresh food for her, the exact same feed she had yesterday and every day of her life before that.

Also, cows don't need to be entertained. For animals that don't sleep, a long, lonely night might be hard to take. Not for a cow. If you should pop in the barn late at night you would find the cows occupied with a variety of activities. When not eating, drinking, chewing their cuds or just dozing, there is always staring at the wall, playing piggyback or even gazing out toward the driveway on the odd chance that they can watch someone stealing gas.

Yes, cows are easily satisfied, so much so, in fact, that they may replace dogs as man's best friend!

## HUSTLING HEIFERS

Our heifers got out recently. It was an accident. Of course, whenever the heifers get out, it's always an accident. Nobody lets heifers loose on purpose. Corralling several yearling heifers running helter-skelter around the farmstead looks impossible at a first glance. It would be easier to refold a road map in the dark or un-mash potatoes. As with lion taming, it is important to remain calm, decide what is possible, and then take immediate steps to avoid further damage.

A gate to their yard was left open, but several heifers were still in the barn, oblivious to the opportunity to frolic. We promptly locked these naïve gals in. The next step was to round up as many of the errant animals as possible, in hopes of moving them unwittingly in a group toward the gate to their yard, before they realized what was happening. Believe it or not, this technique actually works. some of the time. Most of the time, however, only a few heifers can be tricked into returning to their yard en masse. leaving some stragglers who must be cajoled, cornered, and chased back to their safe, secure and familiar home, one at a time.

Because heifers move faster and more unpredictably than mature cows, heifers only get out during mud season. This slows down their pursuers and insures maximum damage to lawns and gardens. While researching easier ways to get heifers back in during mud season, I found two ideas worthy of further consideration.

One is to perfect an invisible fence, using a buried line that would give the heifers a harmless tickle if they were tempted to stray from their secure environs. It works for dogs, why not for heifers? Of course, the charge would have to be much stronger for larger animals, possibly strong enough to knock me out if I stepped over the line. Therefore, my second idea perhaps holds more promise.

What is needed is a pleasingly palatable pellet that, upon consumption, turns a confused, stubborn animal into a docile, pliant pet that follows you anywhere. These pellets would have to be kept in a secure place when not needed, or else you would always be looking over your shoulder and playing the role of the pied piper.

Maybe the easiest solution is to keep the gates shut in the first place.

# KINDS OF KICKS

After 30 years of being kicked by over 600 cows I have come to the conclusion that in spite of the many imaginative ways a cow can lift and put down her rear feet, really, there are only four kinds of kicks.

The first is a slow, gently lifting of the foot. The movement can be forward or backward, side-to-side, or, in its advanced form, can actually be a circular motion as if stirring a huge barrel of pancake batter. This first one is called a "STOPPIT" and usually is used by the cow to indicate mild displeasure with your milking routine.

The second kick is a little more vigorous and quite a bit faster. It is typified by a rapid rearward motion, usually without warning and with enough force to smash a weigh jar. Called a "WATCHIT", it can be a real test of your patience.

The third I call an "OW" or, in extreme cases, an "OWDAMIT." This one requires the cow to instantaneously lift at least one rear foot very high, push it forward and then bring it down as fast as a speeding bullet, pinning your hand, arm or head beneath it.

The last is really a combination of the first three but with enough force and speed to destroy a state of the art milker in less than a millisecond. Affectionately designated by the five letters, "OUSOB," its occurrence is usually followed by a trip to the local commission sale.

Actually, cows are really very gentle, affectionate animals that only use kicking as a means of

communication.    It's just that I would rather they used a
cellular phone.

# Chapter 5

## SO YOU WANT TO LIVE IN THE COUNTRY

While mowing the field near the county road late one afternoon I was amazed at the number of my neighbors I saw returning from their nine to five jobs. They really have the best of both worlds. They can live in the beautiful and unspoiled rural countryside and yet make a good living by commuting to the centers of commerce and industry.

If only I could tell them how lucky they are to be living in the midst of so many active dairy farms. What would I say? What advice would I give them? I probably would say that a farmer, to succeed, has to do certain things at specific times, and that sometimes these essential practices might interfere a teensy-weensy bit with their lifestyle.

I would tell them to relax, enjoy the country air and understand that on occasion they might have to slalom between the dollops of manure left in the road by an over-full manure spreader.

I would tell them that at times they might find themselves following a tractor pulling an unloading wagon at eleven miles per hour and weaving all over the road like a drunken sailor. Again, I would say, be patient, for God's bountiful harvest must be brought back to the home farm for storage so that the cows can keep up the flow of that river of milk so essential to our health. Be comforted by the knowledge that the poor farmer driving that tractor at 5:30 p.m. will have to get two more loads before he milks his cows and that he will not get into the house until after 9 p.m., just in time to hear those dreaded words, "Your supper is in the microwave."

For those fortunate enough to live next to a dairy farm, I would remind them how blessed they are to be able to watch calves frolicking on fresh pasture or to see just milked cows grazing at twilight and to enjoy the tranquil beauty of red gambrel roofed barns trimmed in white or tall blue towers with American flags on them.

For all of this and much more, I would caution them not to be too upset if they should wake up some night to the sound of a herd of buffalo-size bovines charging across their newly seeded, but rain soaked lawn, shredding everything in their path, including flower beds and small dogs.

# MANURE MANAGEMENT

The efficiency gained by housing dairy cattle in free stalls rather than in conventional barns is amazing. Modern farm mechanization allows one man to feed, clean and milk large numbers of cows with very little backbreaking manual labor. That's the upside. The downside is manure handling.

The hardest thing about cleaning a conventional barn is trying to look busy after you have pushed the barn cleaner START button. Not so with a free stall. Moving the darned stuff toward the push off is harder than putting toothpaste back into the tube. It is sort of like pushing smoke down a cat's throat with a darning needle. Anyway, getting "it" into the spreader is only half the battle.

The next challenge is getting to the field without spilling any. One of my new suburban neighbors says farmers are true optimists. They are the only people he knows who put a semi-liquid in a three-sided box, then go up hill and not expect anything to run out the back. He came to this conclusion after driving through thousands of spills on the road near his house.

This spillage can be prevented when carrying the load downhill by steadily speeding up enough to stay ahead of the wave that forms on the surface of the load. If you do spill any in the road be prepared to wash a few neighbors' cars.

When you finally do get your load to the field it only takes one flick of a hydraulic lever to drop all four tons of manure on an area the size of the average two-car garage.

That is, all but the last two inches in the bottom, which takes forever for those little bars to push it out the back. Even longer if it is really cold and the wind is blowing. And longer yet if you forgot your gloves.

Yes, manure really is nature's fertilizer. I just wish that Mother Nature would take care of spreading it herself.

# FARM MACHINERY

Sometimes I think that farming is just a matter of seeing how much you can get done between breakdowns. It seems like I have enough machinery to farm a thousand acres, but only enough actually works to farm 50 acres. In operating farm machinery the most important rule to remember is, "Never let a machine know that you are in a hurry." To do so only invites disaster. However, if a breakdown should occur, here are some tips that may help.

If at first you don't succeed, try a bigger hammer. And if all else fails, use the cutting torch. Keep in mind that if you use the largest hammer first, you get to go to town sooner for parts. Also, the greasier your hands are, the more your nose will itch. It is important that a crescent wrench be well balanced as it will be used as a hammer over fifty percent of the time.

Did you ever notice that all nuts appear to be 1/2 inch? In reality, they are either 9/16" or 7/16". This is done with mirrors. And remember that a tractor which is running poorly will do more work than one which is torn apart. Haying equipment never breaks down in the winter when you have time to fix it. If need be, diesel fuel will defy the law of gravity to enable it to run into your armpit when you are draining a fuel filter.

Just because I have the phone number of the repair shop memorized, I don't want anyone to think that I am not skilled at repairing farm machinery. Actually, I have mastered the most important farm machinery repairing skill: check writing.

# THE ERRANT WAGON

Things were going too well.  By late afternoon we were ahead of schedule, having chopped several loads of haylage from rented land over three miles away.  But then carelessness set in.  Hitching and unhitching the wagons from the truck was much faster if I didn't insert the safety spring lock in each draw pin.  What a time saver that was!

As if to tempt fate, I started for the field one last time, shooting down the hill faster than usual, only to see in my rear view mirror that my wagon was about to pass me.  It would have, too, if it hadn't run out of road.  Words cannot describe the sight of seeing a nearly new huge forage wagon go willingly over an embankment and almost instantly tip over.  There it sat on its side, maybe ten feet below the road, with one wheel still spinning.  After the initial shock wore off, I stopped at my neighbor's to see if I could cut their fence to get the wagon out.

Bless their souls!  They took one look and, with the optimism of successful farmers everywhere, said, "No need to cut the fence, we'll just tip it back on its wheels and pull it up out of there," which they proceeded to do as quickly and easily as an experienced surgeon removes a gall bladder, only a lot faster and with a lot less blood.  I'm so thankful for great neighbors.

During this whole operation, however, a strange thing happened.  Not so strange really, knowing how curious the human animal is.  Cars began to stop so their occupants could observe the catastrophe first hand.  Many offered to help, but most came to apply that ageless principle of exchanging sympathy for details. Before we were finished it was obvious that the word had gotten out. People came from a ten-mile radius to see the mess firsthand.    Soon we had collected more carloads of spectators than the average drive-in movie, all because I was too lazy to use a safety spring pin when I hooked the wagon to the truck.

# MILKING PARLOR

Why do they call that specialized room for milking cows a milking parlor? It could be called a milk room, except that that term is reserved for the area where the fresh milk is cooled and stored. It could be called the "specialized room just for milking, full of expensive pipes and gadgets," but that would be too lengthy.

But why "parlor?" When I think of the word parlor I think of formality, luxury, and pleasant fragrances. These are the last things that you will find in a busy milking parlor. The only formality about a milking parlor is the black and white attire of the Holstein cows. And most milking parlors are not luxurious. Austere would be a better word. Just the necessities. All that really is needed is a machine for every cow, plenty of paper towels, and a place to set the milk and cookies. Pleasant fragrances are rare in a milking parlor. It's not that cows are intentionally odoriferous; it just comes naturally for them. For animals that are always sniffing of something, cows certainly don't smell very good.

To me, the word parlor reminds me of the formal parlor in my childhood home. It had a fireplace with an ornate mantel and beautiful moldings around the doors and windows; it was full of furniture and carpets reserved for special company or for entertaining. I remember celebrating Christmas and family birthdays in that beautiful old parlor.

Among dictionary definitions is a reference to a parlor as a business establishment, often with special equipment or furnishings for personal services, such as a beauty parlor or, better yet, an ice cream parlor. We surely use specialized equipment and, in a sense, offer a personal service to our cows. The big question is, do they appreciate this service? They sure do! On the mornings that I oversleep there is always a group of angry bovines anxiously waiting their turn to receive my personal service.

I'll always remember the plush and formal parlor of my childhood, but somehow I can't picture a herd of cows tromping through there, six at a time.

# TRENCH SILOS

I dug my first trench silo over three decades ago. I had outgrown my one small, concrete, knuckle-busting, knee-scraping upright silo. Thus began my love/hate relationship with horizontal silage storage.

As I freeze my fingers loading the mixer-wagon all winter, I keep telling myself that horizontal silos are the most economical way to store and feed large volumes of silage. A trench silo saves me the time I would otherwise spend fighting with a balky silo unloader, allowing me more time to service and repair my front-end loader, which leads me to another advantage of a trench silo.

An upright silo requires a costly, complicated, and hard to install machine to unload it, a machine which can't be used for anything else, ever. But my tractor-mounted front-end loader not only fills the mixer wagon, but also can plow snow, move firewood or get cats out of trees. Also, trench silos are more flexible when it comes to volume. You literally can put as much silage in a trench as you can stack outdoors.

The things I hate most about trenches are the discarded auto tires that hold the temporary plastic covers in place. Hundreds of tires must be thrown on top of the silo the day you finish filling it. These tires, stacked haphazardly beside the trench for months on end, contain enough rainwater to drown a small elephant. As the tires are hurled, the water swirls around like a boomerang, shooting out to drench you in smelly, dirty, year-old water.

By the time you finish tossing tires you look, feel, and smell like a drowned woodchuck. Then, all year, as you feed the silage out, those same vengeful tires fall one by one into the fresh silage and must be picked up and cast up on the banks of the trench again. By spring, each tire has been handled at least twice, wetting you down each time.

Nevertheless, I still prefer a trench to an upright. Although they are easier to fill, provide more uniform feed, and adapt easily to changes in volume, the real reason I prefer horizontal storage facilities is my maniacal fear of heights. The only way I can fall with a trench silo is to trip getting off the loader tractor.

# THE OUTHOUSE

By now almost a whole generation of farm people have grown up without experiencing the joys and triumphs of using an outhouse. Up until fifty years ago indoor plumbing was not that common on many farms.

The outhouse (or privy, if you're from Maine) was usually a small detached building strategically located close enough to the house to be convenient in winter but far enough downwind so as not to be annoying during the summer. Many outhouses had three holes of varying sizes to accommodate family members of all ages and breadth of beam. The seats were best if made from boxwood that made them velvety-smooth and free from cracks that could be very painful at the worst possible times. Sometimes the wind blew hard enough to make your necktie stand out straight, which is why all the holes had wooden lids that, in our case, looked a lot like ends from apple crates.

I think that the use of corncobs for toilet paper is a myth perpetrated by strapping young men trying to preserve their macho image. Actually, I have fond memories of passing the time leafing through old Sears catalogs, then tearing out the softer pages and crinkling them into a ball, only to smooth them out again, a tenderizing process known to many generations of farm people. Soon all that was left of the catalog were the glossy pages, which were as useless as a chocolate teapot.

One of the perils of using a hole that was too big was the ever-present danger of falling in. The best advice I got on what to do if I were ever unfortunate enough to actually "fall in" came from my father. Obviously, since help would be needed to be extricated, I was told to yell "Fire, fire," because if I yelled what I was actually into, the chances were good that no one would come!

# GREENHOUSES

Just when you think you have everything figured out, something new comes along. Take raising calves, for instance. First it was box stalls, then hutches, and then super hutches. Could they leave it alone? Oh, no! Now the latest trend is keeping calves in - are you ready for this - greenhouses. That's right, plastic, translucent, wind-whipping, pipe-framed structures better suited to housing chrysanthemums than calves.

This trend was started by a clever, insightful, innovative, and cheap farmer searching for an affordable way to house more calves. The use of plastic greenhouses to house livestock is catching on so fast that before anyone realizes what a silly idea this is, most dairy farms will resemble the FTD florist. After all, greenhouses were meant for plants, not animals. If God had wanted animals in them, he would have said so.

The only way I can see to make these delicate plastic structures practical is to find alternate uses for them in addition to their calf-raising function. Since all animals give off some heat, it would be very easy to raise flowers and vegetables in these houses during the colder months.

Because each pen is separated and there is a readily available source of heat and light, I propose a high protein, high-moisture, easily digested vine crop be developed to grow between each calf, so growing calves could browse at their leisure. This would reduce chore time immensely, make the calves largely self-sufficient, and require only occasional visits to make sure the calves were still there. Any unused space could be used for raising poinsettias for Christmas, lilies at Easter and geraniums for Mother's Day. Even tomatoes for fresh homemade salsa are a possibility.

Now that I think about it, this new fad isn't such a silly idea after all.

# MY OFFICE

Most farmers have their offices in their homes. This makes it very convenient to keep up with the never-ending stream of paperwork they face. For me, it is too convenient. My office is just off the kitchen. The only time I get to sit down at my desk is after dark following a long day's work. Not only that, but it is only steps from the refrigerator and the cookie jar. This location makes it difficult for me to work very long between breaks.

My productivity is further hampered by an innate desire to save everything! This usually isn't a problem until I run out of space. In my little office this happened two years ago. Sometimes just getting down to the top of my desk takes much sorting and tossing. At first glance, my desk looks like a paper recycler's dream, but actually, it is a refined, practical and low-cost filing system, for I, and only I, know how far down in which stack the particular item I want is located.

My motto is "Those proud of keeping an orderly desk will never know the thrill of finding something thought irretrievably lost."

Just last Sunday I was determined to spend the afternoon organizing my office once and for all. So, after a big lunch, I went directly into my office, shut the door and worked uninterrupted until my wife woke me up to tell me it was time for dinner.

# REAL FARM KIDS

There was a time when farm kids, called hicks or hayseeds, were teased and taunted by classmates. Not anymore. Today's farm-reared youth are streetwise, industrious, computer-literate entrepreneurs whose farm experience has prepared them far better for the real world than their bored, mall-prowling classmates.

For one thing, real farm kids know how to work. They've learned that if it is their job, they must stick with it until it is finished. On a farm, whining and excuses just don't cut it.

Farm kids know how to make things work long enough to get the job done. Whether it is slipping belts on a vacuum pump or a balky hay rake, whatever happens, farm kids can handle it.

It is this practical ability, honed by years of breakdowns at chore time, that insures that no matter what happens, a farm kid will almost always return from the field with an empty manure spreader. They surprise themselves with how much ingenuity they can muster when faced with the thought of pitching off a full spreader!

Farm kids soon learn to set priorities, a skill few grown-ups master. They look at the big picture, decide what's most important and then tackle those tasks first. Fixing the hole in the heifer fence must come before washing the parlor floor, they realize.

Chores have to be done before playing and fair projects must be completed by opening day. Realizing this, farm kids become excellent time managers. They don't miss deadlines or get taken by surprise very often.

But sound money management is perhaps the most important skill farm kids learn better than their non-farm classmates. It is a frugality born of hard work and saving for a major purchase.

After saving a calf's life or nursing a cow back to health, real farm kids learn that material possessions aren't as important as having a set of values based on a caring and supportive family and experiences that many non-farm youth will never have.

All of these triumphs and frustrations make today's farm youth so much better prepared to face the world, whatever it may bring. Today's hicks and hayseeds are those kids fortunate enough to be raised on a farm.

# Chapter 6

# BARGAINS

Those of us who spend our lives searching for bargains are addicted to endlessly combing through classified ads in farm papers. As in any quest, the search is more exciting than the actual find. Like the gambler at the slot machine anticipating a big win, we hope to find the perfect farm machine, drastically under-priced, in excellent condition, and close to home. Unfortunately, the gambler seldom wins and we rarely meet all three of our criteria.

If it is close to home, it is not cheap. If it's under-priced. it's not in excellent shape, and if it is in excellent shape and under-priced you can bet it is not close to home.

The one thing I have learned from a lifetime of reading the classified section is to interpret some of the key phrases the seller has included to entice you to buy. For example, when the ad says the machine is field ready, that's probably where you will find it. When it says "many new parts," it means the owner has sunk enough money into this looser and it is time to unload it. If it says, "looks good" it probably won't run. It if says runs good, it probably looks terrible. If it says "used less than 800 hours," it should say, "It was in the shop too much to use it any more than that."

When the ad says, "used only one season," the owner is saying, "We were lucky to make it that far." Watch out for the ones that say "Needs TLC," which really means,

"You aren't going to be using that machine for a long, long time."

I've also noticed, in the "Wanted to Buy" section, someone looking for used concrete stave silos. Maybe I'm just getting old, but that sounds like an awful lot of work. It's a wonder someone isn't looking for a used farm pond to move. Probably just another bargain hunter like me.

# WHITE PAILS

There are many essential ingredients to make a farm run smoothly. While good soil and healthy animals help, there really is one item without which a farm could not operate. Of course, I'm talking about the "white plastic pail." Once containing everything from ice cream flavorings to wallboard spackle, these now empty five gallon pails have become one of agriculture's unsung heroes.

Farm uses for these handy buckets fall into two categories: when they are upside down, and when they are right side up. Bottom side up, they make an excellent step stool if one needs to replace a light bulb, scrub a low ceiling, or see over everyone's head at an auction. Other uses for inverted pails include protecting early tomato transplants, covering aboveground well casings, and hiding cats from unfriendly dogs.

The uses for these pails when right side up are virtually limitless. In the milk house we use ours for storing colostrum, mixing milk replacer and warming the teat dip jug on below zero mornings. They are essential for carrying water to fresh cows, weaned calves, and steaming radiators.

Not all the uses around the farm are traditional. We use white pails for a moisture and manure proof temporary tool-box for repair jobs in the free stall area, collecting forage samples for moisture testing, and draining the pool filter. In the garden these containers are great for carrying fertilizer, watering plants, and lugging in the zucchini.

Around the house these pails are excellent for storing wool for braided rugs, as indestructible toy boxes, and as planters for Christmas trees. The downside to white pails is that now we keep much more stuff than we would if our only storage containers were rapidly deteriorating cardboard boxes. Our old milk house is filled with pails half full of treasures such as obsolete plumbing parts, caked fertilizer, and bent nails. It is hard to imagine life without white plastic pails. That would be almost as terrifying as life without duct tape.

# ON WEARING GLASSES

To most people, wearing glasses is merely an inconvenience. To a farmer it is a pain on the nose. I guess the only reason I wear glasses is to see where I'm going. Inevitably, as one matures, the time comes when the arms aren't long enough to read fine print, like newspaper headlines, and the wearing of glasses becomes necessary to do any fine work such as opening a car door or navigating a mall parking lot.

Cleanliness is the big problem. Most of the time my glasses have been splashed with enough blood, milk, water and diesel fuel so that my glimpse of the world resembles the view as seen through the bottom of a nearly empty peanut butter jar. Frequent cleaning would be easy in a pristine environment, but on a farm it is nearly impossible. Rubbing them on your coveralls just makes matters worse. A clean linen handkerchief would be best, if only I hadn't just wiped off a grease fitting with mine. I recommend the tail of a flannel shirt, preferably your own.

Why is it when you can't see far away, you're called near sighted? Unfortunately, I need help to focus both near and far - I guess that's why bifocals were invented. "What are bifocals?" you may ask.

They are a miraculous device allowing one to alternately focus on near and distant objects and feel dizzy and insecure all at the same time, especially when descending stairs. As you can see, I have a dim view of wearing glasses, but I must admit that they offer some protection from flying wood and metal chips.

In the winter glasses also allow you to run plumb into a wall when they fog up after coming in from the cold. Wearing glasses is kind of like farming, sometimes you can see where you are going and sometimes you can't.

# ADVERTISING

Change is difficult for anyone to accept, especially farmers. If you know how hard it is to change yourself, then you realize how hard it is for others to change. We cling to our tried and true ways, afraid to take risks, to innovate, and perhaps improve our lot in life.

Often change is forced upon us by circumstances beyond our control. Ever-rising costs and stagnant prices have forced many farmers to seek new ways to enhance revenues.

Why not capitalize on a farm's natural attributes by selling advertising space for consumer products? While "DRINK MILK" signs on barns are common, there are many innovative, cutting edge ways to gain much needed cash simply by trying something new. For example, the tailgates on silage trucks and forage wagons could carry news of super market specials, tips for drivers, new and used car ads, and directions on how to perform the Heimlich maneuver, since most drivers have ample time to read while following one of these slow-moving vehicles.

Another way to enhance farm income is to accept sponsorships for your farm. The company logo would appear on all employee uniforms, proclaiming for all to see that this was the official work boot, coverall, laundry detergent, and aftershave of your farm.

Or perhaps one could rent ad space on the sides of cows pastured near busy highways, although for enough money, a farmer would surely jump at the chance to have his cows repainted so that all of the cows had identical designs, for example, in the shape of a popular athletic logo.

Each summer as the zucchini wars begin, advertising messages could be written on the sides of these delicious vegetables, which are then left on porches much the same way newspapers are.   The streets could be full of zucchini boys delivering promotional messages in residential areas all over America.

The advertising potential of cow manure has not been fully explored.   This much-maligned treasure of fertility and fragrance could be utilized as a new form of crop art by spelling words and making designs in the snow with the manure spreader or writing messages to promote air travel and balloon rides.  If you have other advertising ideas, you may contact me at peckhaven@cowflop.moo.com.

# WARM HANDS

Happiness may be wine, women and song to some people, but for me happiness is a new pair of work gloves. Working on a farm in the winter without warm hand protection is as unbearable as living in Florida in the summer.

Just the thought of purchasing a new pair of work gloves conjures up visions of row upon row of gauntlets of all kinds and description. I say purchase, because gloves, like spouses, must be selected personally. Never let someone else choose either for you.

It is important to realize that no matter how many choices you have, there is no such thing as "perfect" gloves. If they are insulated enough to keep your fingers warm on a frigid day, they are too thick to grasp anything smaller than a tractor steering wheel. If they are limber enough so you can unsnap a gate chain, your fingers will freeze the minute you leave the warm milk house.

After trying on every glove in the store, I usually settle on leather-faced gloves with a cloth back that looks like it was made from old mattress ticking. Just trying on gloves is a joy. I love the soft warm lining touching my fingers for the first time, the leather palm wrinkling when I flex my fingers, and the soft knit cuff caressing my wrist. Life just doesn't get much better than this.

But, alas, there is a down side to new work gloves. As wonderful as they look and feel, they must be treated like a new car that hasn't yet received its first scratch. The nemesis of leather gloves is water. On a farm it is a real chore to keep new gloves from getting wet. To that end, I often find myself sweeping snow from a tractor seat with my bare hands, just to keep my gloves dry!

It is a little known fact that when wet, leather-palmed gloves dry out they are harder than a three day-old bagel. Stiff leather gloves are not a pretty sight, so keeping them dry becomes a preoccupation that makes an otherwise dull day seem to fly by. Nevertheless, I would rather have a new pair of gloves than either wine or song.

# VACATIONS

The common perception is that farmers work too hard and don't take enough time off to enjoy life. Not me. I take off every chance I get. I always have and I think every farmer should. Life is just too short to work all the time.

I think my family has, over the years, enjoyed our many trips and adventures, all financed by our bathroom fund. You see, we have always intended to remodel our old bathroom. We started saving toward this goal many times, only to spend our meager bathroom fund on another family vacation.

As a family we visited Disneyland and toured the many sites in our nation's Capital. We saw the U.S. Naval Academy at Annapolis and relived colonial life at Williamsburg. We watched the spouting of Yellowstone's Old Faithful and gazed in awe at the beauty of Mount Rushmore. We saw New York State from the mighty Niagara Falls to the scenic splendor of the Adirondacks. We never did get our bathroom remodeled. Was this the right thing to do? I think so.

Yes, farmers do work hard, but they should never lose sight of the fact that this precious time the family spends together can never be replaced. All too soon the children are grown and off on their own and the opportunity to travel and spend time together as a family is gone. This fact must have weighed heavily upon my younger daughter's mind during her first term of college

for, after being away for many months, she called home
one night just to thank us for taking all those wonderful
family trips. She knew we had financed those trips with
the money we had saved for a new bathroom. That's why
she thanked us by saying, "I'm glad we never got our
bathroom remodeled. I just can't imagine calling home to
say thanks for having such a nice bathroom."

# BIOTECHNOLOGY

There is great concern in some circles about the safety of G.M.O.'s. Since I seem to spend most of my time going in circles, I am the perfect one to clear up misconceptions about this relatively new technology. So, just what is a G.M.O?

No, it's not a first cousin to an H.M.O., nor does it stand for Great Men Overeat. When you combine the genetic material of two different organisms to improve their resultant productivity or disease resistance without materially changing the plant or seed, you have a Genetically Modified Organism (G.M.O.). In the last few years many seeds have become available that are resistant to specific insects and diseases. This scientific breakthrough enables farmers to improve their crop yields while using less expensive and less harmful pesticides and herbicides.

So, what's the problem? Well, some groups are very concerned about the effects these modified seeds might have on the environment in the long-term. Yet most scientists seem to think these modifications are safe and will prove to be another of the many advances in agriculture in the last 200 years to grow better animals, seeds, and food crops.

Speaking of long-term effects, isn't it odd that some technological improvements are readily adopted with little or no concern for the long-term? Where would we be if we had waited to see what the long-term consequences would be before the widespread adoption of cell phones, ATM machines, and polyester pants? We would still be shouting at each other, carrying large wads of bills, and mending and ironing our cotton pants, that's where!

As for genetic modification, mankind has been doing that since the beginning of time. What's the big deal? Every time we select a spouse who is smarter and better looking than we are, we do so in the hope that our children will be both prettier and more intelligent, and usually they are. At least until they become teenagers.

Genetic modification is proving very beneficial in the medicinal and pharmacological field where its use may save lives. Maybe people will feel differently about biotechnology when the only treatment for their medical problem is a G.M.O. Maybe G.M.O should stand for Genetically Modified Opportunities. Can't you picture sweet corn without pesky silks or green beans that self-destruct on your dinner plate, so that you don't have to eat them?

# THE METRIC SYSTEM

At one time we were supposed to convert to the metric system in this country. Major economic benefits were supposed to result from this conversion because nobody would have any idea how much anything cost.

Take livestock salt for example. Now salt is sold in convenient units of measure called "bags." However, under the metric system, if I were to buy salt at my local farm supply store (it starts with "A"), the clerk might say, "What size do you want, the 5 kilo or the 26 hectare?" While I was trying to decide, the clerk would say sharply, "Hurry up, my lunch break starts in five liters." I would wind up buying enough salt to last four years, which would be great for the economy.

As soon as highway signs started to go up saying, "Fourteen centipedes to the next exit," open-minded Americans started using them for target practice. Other than the 9-millimeter bullet, the metric system never caught on in this country, but it did in Canada. That's why when they give the temperature as nine degrees on a Canadian radio station and you ask several Canadians how cold it really is, you will get answers all the way from, "I think it's around 30" to "I haven't the slightest idea."

I certainly wouldn't want to live in a country where no one knows how cold it really is.

# REST SAFELY

Because farming is one of the most hazardous occupations, farmers have to be safety conscious every waking moment. A recent article on farm safety pointed out that most farm accidents occur late in the day, especially for people over fifty. This clearly illustrates the need for us post semi-centenarians (those over 50) to regularly take a short nap at lunchtime. If practiced properly and regularly, a midday rest would avoid both fatigue and stress.

What a godsend this article was. I've been looking for years for an acceptable excuse to lie down for a few moments after lunch. In the past, the minute my head hit the white lace pillow on the sofa I began to feel guilty about wasting valuable time. Now when I stretch out midday on the couch, in my barn clothes, I'll be secure in the knowledge that I will be both reducing stress and preventing fatigue later in the day.

At this point a few tips on how to properly take a nap are in order. First, the house must be reasonably quiet. A short but boring piece of reading material should be close at hand. A recent market report or an extension newsletter will do. Next, to insure that your nap is merely a short respite in an otherwise exciting and productive day, place the receiver for the cordless phone within arm's reach. My experience has been that no matter when you break for lunch, early or two hours late, as soon as you've fallen into a wonderfully deep, crisis-forgetting, paradise-achieving state of slumber, the phone will ring. Sometimes I weave the phone's beeping into the plot of my dream, but usually I wake up and fumble for the receiver, only to hear a hesitant voice extolling the virtues of some product whose representative will be in the neighborhood tomorrow and would I like to make an appointment. I usually just thank them for the wake up call and indicate that no one here speaks English so a sales call would be worthless. It's at this point you never lie back down. The next telemarketing call may not come for hours.

A post nap ritual of straightening up the sofa so it looks like no one was there is a necessity. Then put your shoes on and get out of the house as quickly as possible before the guilt sets in.

Besides relieving stress and preventing fatigue, a well organized noon nap will leave you prepared for your second eight hour day.

# Chapter 7

# WEATHER

What is it with these TV weather people anyway? Why do they make the weather so dramatic? Farmers, like so many others, rely on accurate, up-to-date forecasts of what Mother Nature will bring in the next few days. Very important business and personal decisions are dependent on this crucial information.

Questions that all farmers face, like whether to clean the heifer yard before it snows, move that wood to the cellar before it rains or just chuck it all and go skiing tomorrow, are all contingent on forecasts presented by a grinning, cheerful airhead whose idea of happiness is a sunny weekend followed by a rainy Monday. For some reason, they spend their whole workweek looking forward to the weather on the weekend. Sometimes I feel like shouting at the TV, "Hey, what about the rest of us lunkheads who work all week long and need to know what the weather will be like Monday through Friday!"

These TV personalities really bug me. They don't even know what the word 'cold' means. In October they say it is cold when the temperature drops into the 30's. Then in January cold will describe temperatures below zero. In March cold is in the mid 20's. Can't they ever make up their minds?

And then there are the wind-chill factors. Every time I turn the radio on they announce the temperature as 30 below with the wind-chill. All summer long no one mentions wind-chill. It seems like every winter the weather people suddenly come up with wind-chill factors to make winter more dramatic. Why don't they use the same system in the summer? You never hear them say, "It is 98° in the sun, but with the wind-chill factor it only feels like 76°."

Why do they try to make the weather so dramatic? Why is it that when there is an uneventful weather day here the grinning weather person must find sensational weather somewhere else to report. Like Montana getting 18 feet of snow in 35 minutes or a tornado touching down on every trailer park in Florida.

It is too bad that they put forth so much effort to make the weather dramatic, yet they seldom get it right.

# I HATE WINTER!

I hate winter. I hate the bitter cold, the never-ending battle with the woodpile, the walks to be shoveled, the blasts of cold air every time the parlor doors swing open and the constant fight with brittle, frozen machines just waiting for the most inopportune time to break. The most maddening thing about winter is that it really isn't necessary. Winter only exists because those Romans who invented our calendar needed something to keep fall and spring from fighting. The silly part is that we have been going along with this unbelievable strategy for centuries because nobody has had courage enough to point this out to calendar-makers.

If I ever get elected to a position of power, the first thing I will do is reorganize the calendar. It's really not that hard. Just add a month to fall and a month to spring. That means that winter would only be one month long. Now that's more like it since everyone knows half the time winter weather is really quite nice. That leaves only two weeks of really bad weather. I'll toast to that.

What really frosts me about winter is the time it takes to go to the bathroom when you are wearing a heavy coat, insulated vest, two pullover sweatshirts, full length coveralls and flannel-lined dungarees. By the time I get undressed I have forgotten why I came in the house in the first place.

# SNOW

Snow, beautiful snow. Isn't it amazing how the fluff we look forward to in November turns into the stuff we dread in January, grow to hate in February and openly despise by March?

Years when the total snowfall is above normal (and even normal is too much), coping with each new snowfall is about as much fun as peeling an apple in the dark. More than a foot of snow at one time means several hours on the tractor just doing a minimal job of "plowing out." That's time we could have spent scrubbing the milk house walls, making important management decisions or, better yet, taking a nap.

After several such storms, just finding places to put the snow becomes a monumental headache. Our tractor scoop can only pile the snow so high, after that we must look for new places to push, pile and hide it. By March our yard looks like a series of Civil War earthworks, higher than an elephant and some actually resembling an elephant, trunk and all. Traces of these carcasses will undoubtedly survive well into May.

As spring approaches, the glee we feel in our hearts over winter's demise slowly ebbs away as the reality of mud season gradually sinks in. 'And sink in we do, often up to our shoe tops. Mud is so messy. You can't shake it off your shoes; sometimes you can't even wash it off. Just when you think you have rid your shoes of all traces of the brown dirt, you somehow manage to track some onto the new carpet.

While winter drags on interminably, mud season seems even longer. Then one day, when you least expect it, spring arrives. Birds sing, grass turns green, the sun shines and potholes deepen, in a sudden burst of life dedicated to making us forget all about winter.

The best part about spring is that it is so beautiful, so warm, so magical and so enticing that we easily forget all about snow, mud and cold, as if they never existed and will never come again. But deep down we know that the snow-covered elephants will return.

# HOLIDAY GREETINGS

'Tis the season to extend greetings to one and all. Often we are too busy and fail to make time for the many people who deserve our special attention during this festive time of year. To those among us who may be forgotten in the hustle and bustle, I offer warmest regards for a safe and happy holiday season.

Merry Christmas to salesmen who make you feel guilty and to milk truck drivers who have lost their directions. We greet with particular warmth people who wake and smell smoke, animal rights activists who have never been on a farm and wives trying out new recipes. A joyous Yule to John Deere owners whose conduct is unworthy of their tractor. Merry Christmas to people who monopolize the question and answer period at meetings and those who talk during movies.

Greetings to people who can't find their glasses and to farmers with frozen manure spreaders. Happy Holidays to tellers who have made a mistake in addition, to girls who have made a mistake in judgment and to all those who can't eat clams.

A special greeting to veterinarians treating milk fever, mechanics with missing sockets, bankers with frozen assets and A.I. technicians who have holes in their gloves. Merry Christmas to the defeated, the forgotten and the inept.

Best Wishes to all those who think they are in love but aren't sure and those who can't sleep but need to. Greetings to farmers with cold feet, tractors with leaks in their radiators and people doing up bundles with string that's too short. But most of all, a special holiday wish to all those who have to milk cows and do chores on Christmas morning.

# CHRISTMAS LIST

It is hard to believe that a farmer would be sending a Christmas list to Santa Claus in these modern times. That's why I was shocked to find some farmer's wish list mixed in with my e-mail messages recently. Yes, in today's sophisticated technical world, sending a letter to Santa by e-mail is permissible. However, because of this mix-up, Santa may never know what this one farmer really wanted. My only hope is that Santa will read this story and realize what most farmers desire for Christmas.

The list I mistakenly received was unique in that it did not ask for the usual farmer dream gifts like a five-day-cow, a blind milk inspector or odorless cow manure. It did include, however, some items I might add to my Christmas list - things like rhubarb pie-scented teat dip, breakdown insurance and, best of all, a remote tractor starter.

Because farmers work outside in all kinds of weather my gift requests include clothing and footwear to ease chores during the cold winter months to come. Coveralls with a built-in butt warmer are appealing, but potentially dangerous. Boots with retractable ice cleats top my list, with internet access from the tractor cab a close second. Speaking of computers, why can't we get software that would predict the weather better than our present system of using the dog's tail. (If the tail is wet, it is raining, if it is dry, it is not, etc.)

My Christmas list includes glasses that don't fog up when coming in from the cold, a box of instant apple pie powder (they do it with mashed potatoes) and a virtual reality helmet that will allow me to experience the joy and satisfaction of milking my cows without leaving my warm couch in the living room.

As you can easily see, farmers are a humble bunch who don't ask for much, just the impossible.

# NEW YEAR'S DAY

January First marks the beginning of a brand new year. Traditionally it's a time to reflect on the past year, a time to make plans for the future, and, on the farm, a time to wish the New Year started on May first or, better yet, on July first!

The Romans may have been smart enough to develop a calendar, choose some clever names for the months and even figure out how many days each month should have, but their temperate climate let them start the year anytime they wanted.

Now, because of their mistake, we must freeze our ears on the way to New Year's Eve parties and First Night celebrations, and milk on New Year's Day with icicles hanging from our noses, red from too much partying the night before. If New Year's Day fell on July first, these celebrations of a new beginning could be held outside, around a pool, in a gazebo in the park or even on the front lawn.

Of course, with the present system, our New Year's Day is not plagued with mosquitoes or oppressive heat, nor dampened by a sudden violent thunderstorm. Now that I think about it, New Year's without mulled cider or holly and mistletoe would not be the same.

Fortunately, the period from Christmas to New Year's Day is usually very cold, but relatively free of major snow storms. This is either due to an ingrained weather pattern or God's benevolent gift to children everywhere, choosing to save major storms for days when school could be cancelled.

At least this year we won't have to prepare ourselves for a possible Y2K crisis. Last year I was ready for any unforeseen interruption in power, phone service and the Internet. In fact, it took me until Easter to convince my wife that stocking up on root beer and corn chips was a precaution that simply had to be taken.

Actually, I can't wait for New Year's to be over. If I party too much, getting up the next morning gets to be as hard as blowing bubbles in a blizzard. If I don't party enough I might better have stayed home and gone to bed early.

I still think a July First New Year's party would be a blast. So, if you see a group of wistful farmers standing around my pool next summer singing "Auld Lang Syne," you will know why.

# NEW YEAR'S RESOLUTIONS

I had a dream one night that my cows had drawn up a list of New Year's resolutions for them to follow. It read:

1. I will always keep my mouth closed when chewing my cud.
2. No matter how hot it is nor how many flies light on my back, I will not fling silage from the bunk onto my body because that only attracts more flies.
3. No matter how convenient or how tempting, I will not pick my nose with my tongue, especially in front of company.
4. In a spirit of cooperation, from this moment henceforth, I will only poop in the alley and never in my stall or in the milking parlor.
5. To prevent pain to my owner or me I will never step on my own teats, nor those of my herd mates.
6. Out of respect for their years of training and out of gratitude for the free medical care I receive, I will treat my veterinarian with the esteem his profession deserves. I vow to do this despite being examined in some very embarrassing places.
7. Ditto for the artificial breeder.
8. I will always do what I am told, or at least what I think I'm being told or what it looks like I'm being told to do.
9. I will eat willingly and with great gusto whatever feed is put before me and will not snuffle it all around trying to find one mouthful that is better than all the others.

10.  I promise not to spend my leisure time searching for
open gates.  If, however, I should discover one and find
myself outside the barn, I will confine my explorations to
the driveway and will not under any condition go running
across a rain-soaked lawn, nor destroy any vegetables in the
garden, except possibly the string beans or a few zucchini.
11.  And lastly, I promise to stay away from the swimming
pool, especially on really hot days when a dip would be so
refreshing.

I was so impressed with their thoughtful promises
to do better this year, that I immediately nailed the
resolutions to the milk house wall for all to see.
Unfortunately, the hammering woke me up.

# CABIN FEVER

I never owned a tractor with a cab, but I always wanted to, particularly when I was spreading manure in January with a north wind blowing snow in my face, numbing my cheeks and caking my eyebrows with ice. Someday, I kept telling myself, I am going to sit in my own airtight, heated and air-conditioned paradise, oblivious to the weather swirling around me. However, spreading manure daily with a cableless tractor does give one a better appreciation of the hardships pioneers experienced crossing the American plains in the winter, and they did it without live hydraulics or power steering.

Well, it finally happened. We had the opportunity to buy a four-wheel drive tractor with a beautiful, heated, air-conditioned, and nearly soundproof cab. We told ourselves that we really needed the four-wheel drive to avoid getting "stuck" during the awkward mud season between winter and when it is dry enough to plow. To justify buying a toy of this size and cost we made a list of all the places where the added traction of four-wheel drive would be invaluable. Nobody mentioned the palatial cab. That just came along with the deal. We would simply have to accept its heat, air-conditioning and soft, comfortable seat as the price we would pay to get the features we really wanted.

The deal was made; the tractor came and we started making the daily manure run to distant rented fields. The first trip was glorious. No wind in my face, no frozen finger tips and no need for gloves either. It was unbelievably easy. The second trip was so naturally comfortable that I almost dozed off halfway there. By the third trip I was totally bored. There were no challenges. I missed trying to see where I was going through my gloved fingers as I held my hand in front of my face to ward off the frigid wind. This was too easy.

Then I began to notice some things that made me uneasy. I couldn't see things around the tractor as well. The glare of the glass and the posts between them made visual checks much more difficult. Also, I couldn't hear the noises of impending disaster. You know, the sounds of bearings squeaking, belts squealing or the clatter of parts falling off entirely. Why, I wouldn't even be able to smell the smoke of a slipping clutch.

I began to wonder if the protective cocoon of a tractor cab was really worth it. Just then it began to pour. As the sheets of rain bounced off the curved windshield and my heated cabin kept me high and dry, I decided that a cab on a tractor was a great idea after all.

# MUD

I hate mud! All farmers hate mud. They know that a certain amount of rain is necessary for good crop yields but they still hate the mud. It is worse in the early spring when the weather starts to warm and the winter frost begins to leave the ground.

Farm wives also hate the muddy season. To them, spring means lots and lots of dirt tracked into the house on the feet of both young and adult children.

One of life's great mysteries is how a spot in a cornfield can be so wet in early April that a tractor and manure spreader can sink almost out of sight in it and yet, one month later, be so hard that a plow barely bites in more than a few inches.

We have a spot like that which we call "Devil's Hole." Sometimes I think it lies in wait, smug and confident that I'll drive right into the middle of it and be swallowed up - tractor, spreader and all, leaving only the tractor muffler and half the steering wheel sticking out.

That's not the worst part, though, for if "Devils Hole" should devour my tractor, I couldn't pretend that nothing had happened, for you see, "Devil's Hole" is within sight of the road. I couldn't just trudge back to the bam for a chain and another tractor, whistling merrily to myself as my feet gathered enough clay to make several large pots. I just couldn't leave with that mud enshrouded monument to my poor judgment, right there in plain sight.

Yes, I do hate mud.  If only God could find another way to get needed moisture into our fertile soil.

# SPRING

It happens every spring.  As the days get longer and the average daily temperature rises, a strange feeling comes over me.  It starts with an itching in the palms of my hands and is followed by a longing to start the big tractor and hitch it to the plow.   A warm breeze from the south only intensifies the sensation.

Every farmer has experienced it: that urge to drop those plows into the ground, hear the engine roar and the turbo whine and smell that indescribable aroma of unburned diesel fuel.  I call it BLACK SMOKE FEVER.

Only this year it is different.  This year I have been haunted by a recurring dream.  Actually, it is more like a nightmare.  In my fantasy I have just purchased the corn planter of my dreams.  It is the latest design, computerized precision at its best.  I can't wait to try it out.  On the first warm, dry day, well ahead of any of my neighbors, I proudly start for the field.

I can see it now; there I am bursting with pride planting that long field by the road, zooming along, the envy of farmers everywhere.  But, as I approach the fence at the end of the field, I can't stop.  Try as I might, the tractor just keeps going.  The fence is looming closer and closer.  The planter marker catches a fence post and the wire gets tangled in the Teflon-coated press wheels.  As I frantically try to stop the tractor I can see the whole fence being dragged behind me, each post breaking off one by one as the wire tightens, all the way back to the barnyard.  Hopelessly, I watch in horror as the wire pulls tight against the barn and the barn collapses in a huge cloud of dust.

As if this weren't bad enough, it is just at this instant that I notice all of my neighbors watching me from the road. They are just standing there laughing and pointing. I couldn't be more embarrassed, for all farmers know that it is bad enough to do something foolish, but it is far worse to do it within sight of the road.

It is always at this point in my dream that I wake up in a cold sweat. To be sure, I think that I'll plant that long field by the road after dark this year.

# HEAT

If you think the heat of summer bothers you, think how it must aggravate cows.  How would you like to be stuck wearing the same fur coat all summer with no way of taking it off.  In fact, cold weather is less of a hardship for them than hot weather.  They seem to like it best when the temperature is between 30 to 70 degrees.

As the mercury surges beyond 70 degrees the more uncomfortable and less productive cows become.  At 80 degrees they love to stand in the breeze of an electric fan.  At 90 degrees water seems to be the big attraction.  Apparently, some primeval instinct tells her, "Man, it's hot," giving her a clear signal to hog the water fountain, keeping all of her thirsty sisters from enjoying the unending supply of the elixir of life they find so refreshing on blistering days.

Cows are amazingly resourceful.  For each degree above 90, they have a plethora of tactics to draw upon, all skillfully employed at the right moment and designed to invoke sympathy, since cows seem to thrive on making their owner feel guilty.

Sometimes to keep cool, cows will very cleverly, using their mouths as catapults, throw feed all over their backs until they look like a black and white walking feed bunk.  This maneuver seldom works as the accumulated grain particles on their backs attract flies, thus exacerbating their problems.

In addition to the two water fountains, we have added two large galvanized water tubs to give the herd more access to water on hot days.  Unfortunately, two prima donnas are experimenting by standing with their front feet in the trough as if it were a giant bovine wading pool.  Although this gives those two individuals great comfort, their herd mates look upon this as a disgusting habit, akin to 'erping' in the feed bunk.

The truth is, despite several huge electric fans, good barn ventilation and plentiful drinking water, dairy cows really hate 90-degree weather.  There isn't much we can do until their vanity allows them to part with that darn heavy fur coat.

# WATER

It was a good movie. A typical western drama. The pioneer family had left their roots in Boston to make a new life in the west before the turn of the century. They wanted to be farmers in a land dominated by cattle ranches. Fencing in the range brought on the inevitable conflicts between farmers and ranchers.

In this particular story the rancher lived upstream of the creek that ran through the homesteader's property. At one point, in an attempt to drive our heroic family off their land, the rancher damned up the stream, depriving the farmer of water for his family and livestock. Finally, in an emotional, climatic scene, the pioneer wife looses her composure and pleads with her stoic, persevering husband, saying that she wishes they had never left Boston, for she hates life on the lonely prairie. Pointing to the dry streambed, she screams in despair, "We don't even have the essentials of life here!"

All of this time my observant, then five year old daughter, was sitting on my lap, taking in all the splendor, beauty and emotion of the enfolding scene before her. Suddenly she turned to me and whispered, as if to agree with the wife's complaints, "They don't even have a mailbox!"

Yes, water is essential to a farm, but to a five-year-old, so is a mailbox. Maybe she was right. A mailbox is essential. I am fortunate that my mail comes before noon every day so at lunchtime I can sort through piles of letters, bills, catalogs and free shampoo samples. What I enjoy most are checks and meeting notices. I despise junk mail disguised as checks and million dollar sweepstakes entries, reading "Dear Mr. Peckhaven Farm, you may already have won..." It is hard to believe that, with the incredible number of specialty catalogs we receive, Sears and Wards had to give up their catalog sales. We average three a day and sometimes as many as six a day in the weeks before Christmas. Thank goodness we have a wood stove.

In our part of the country we rarely have to worry about availability of water; rather our challenge is how to manage around too much at the wrong times. After driving through the parched western United States, I can see why a bountiful supply of water is essential to farmers there, but to me, and to my daughter, so is a mailbox.

# DROUGHT

For us, this has been the driest year ever. I say that because the second driest year in my memory occurred in my third year of farming. It didn't rain all summer that year, too, but we had had a normal winter and spring, unlike this year's drab, snowless winter and sparse spring rains.

It is amazing what two months without rain will do for what once was a sunny disposition. Watching corn tassel waist high and start to die is not fun. Oh, sure, haying was a snap. No worries about the hay getting rained on. The only problem was there wasn't any hay to cut. Our second cutting was shorter than fuzz on a peach.

I'm reminded of a summer trip we once took through Wyoming. The ranch country was barren and brown, populated only by occasional coarse tufts of an unappetizing-looking grass, except for those areas bordering streams, where lush alfalfa abounded, thanks to irrigation. It became obvious that Wyoming soil was very productive, it just lacked water, something usually plentiful in the northeast.

Right now our lawn is as brown as the Wyoming prairie. A wise sage once said, "We owe our whole existence to the fact that the earth is covered with six inches of top soil and it rains." How true. It takes a year like this to awaken us to this stark reality.

As we watch storm clouds form, darken and then divide and drift around us, we rejoice in the many good things a prolonged drought brings. Not only were we freed from the weekly chore of mowing the lawn but, gardening was much easier. You see, ordinarily one hill of zucchini will supply a whole neighborhood.  In fact, the month of August is the only time we country dwellers lock our doors, so that some kind neighbor won't leave us some zucchini while we are away. It was so dry this summer that not even zucchini would grow.  No one can remember when it was ever that dry.

# WET OR DRY

The old timers used to say, "A dry year may scare you to death, but a wet year will starve you to death." After this year's deluge, I know why.

A dry year lets you plant when ever you want, but there may not be much to harvest. A wet year provides enough precious water to grow a bountiful crop, but the fields are usually too wet to either plant or harvest. In a dry year yields are low but there are more options to find enough feed to last until the next year. In a wet year your only option is to stay inside and listen to those raindrops on the roof, until you slowly go mad.

All this time the guilt-masters at Cornell are hounding you about how the best managers always have their corn planted by the 10$^{th}$ of May and are well into hay harvest by the 20$^{th}$ of that same month. These target dates keep rolling before your tired eyes as you struggle through ankle deep ruts, and that's just in the driveway!

Listening to the weather reports doesn't help either. Some smiling, photogenic, fashionably dressed weather person takes great pride in telling us how fortunate we are to have ample rainfall this spring, because some areas of Florida and western United States are as much as ten inches below normal. It doesn't take many brains to see who is getting all the rain they are not getting. The only good think about a wet year is that we don't have to water the lawn or wash our cars very often.

Many old timers were pretty sharp or they wouldn't have survived to be "old" timers. But the reality is, a wet year will both scare and starve you to death.

# Chapter 8

# MIGRATORY BIRDS OF A DIFFERENT
# SORT

For centuries farmers have marked the arrival of
spring with the return of such migratory birds as the red-
winged blackbird and the robin.   In the same manner,
today's farmers know summer has come with the arrival of
another type of bird.

I call them the southern-accented pick-up bird.  They
are easily identified by the bright colors and shiny chrome
of their trucks.  A sighting of these birds is confirmed by
spotting South Carolina or Georgia on their license plates.

They may be selling anything from bargain shop
tools to complete paint jobs for your buildings.   These
birds are never seen in the colder months in these parts.
Farmers are safe from their visits as long as it is cold
enough that gloves are necessary.

But in the heat of summer these birds arrive, full of
stories of tremendous quality at great savings.  I don't
know where they spend the rest of the year but I can't help
dreaming about what I will do when I retire.

Perhaps I will buy a shiny red pickup, load it with
cheap tools and, come November, head for South Carolina
to enjoy the warm weather while giving those birds the
same opportunity for tremendous quality at great savings.

# WHICH FARMER IS IT?

When you drive into a farmer's yard, you never know which farmer you are going to meet. Will it be an exhilarated farmer who has just delivered a beautiful heifer calf from his best cow or will it be an exasperated farmer who has just explained to a new employee, for the fourth time, how to do some simple task, only to hear that dreaded phrase, "Oh! If that's how you wanted it done, why didn't you just say so?"

Most farmers are many people rolled into one. One minute you are a mechanic repairing an essential machine so it will last long enough to get the job done; the next minute you are answering a call from someone wondering if you have time to answer a few questions.

Is the person who is furious, frustrated and fatigued trying to get a stubborn yearling heifer back through a gate she very easily found in the dark, the same person who patiently comforts a tearful child, upset at the death of a family pet? Can the same person work 16 hour days at planting and harvest time and still remain calm when someone asks, "Just what do you farmers do all winter to keep busy?"

Yes, a farmer can and quite often does, for you see, a farmer is a rare mixture of technical expert, professional manager and amateur animal and people psychologist. If that weren't enough, most farmers are community leaders in addition to being a spouse and parent. They really are many people all rolled into one.

You never know which farmer you will meet, but you can be sure of one thing, he will be polite, and he will be glad to see you, but only as long as you don't take up too much of his valuable time.

# FREE ADVICE

Where do farmers go for sound, unbiased, free advice? Oh, I know that there are consultants who provide advice on record keeping and financial matters for a fee, but where do farmers go for assistance in making those really important decisions like what direction should a business go, what changes would make the business more efficient or even what color farm tractor should be purchased?

Well, I think I have found the answer. When I see another farmer undertaking a change in his business I know exactly what he is doing right, what he is doing wrong and how I would change it. So it occurred to me that farmers get the best advice from other farmers. Since farmers are reluctant to come right out and tell you what is right or wrong, I developed this ingenious plan to get sound. free advice from other farmers.

Simply invite a busload of farmers, preferably from another county, to visit your farm so you can brag about the changes you've made and improvements you've undertaken. Then, just a few minutes before they are scheduled to leave, you excuse yourself, slip into your seed company jacket, pull your hat down over your ears, put on your dark glasses, and sneak onto the bus. They'll think you are just one of the group. The real advice starts to flow when the bus drives off. It never fails. Farmer after farmer will have terrific ideas on what you did wrong, what you did right, what you should change, and what direction you should take. And the best part is, all this advice doesn't cost you anything. The only disadvantage is that you may have to walk home from wherever the bus stops next.

# VETERINARIANS

I have always felt that the real unsung hero of the modern efficient dairy farm was the veterinarian, known affectionately as "the Vet" or even "Doc," when the cow is really sick.

A dairy farm is truly blessed if it is served by a dedicated large animal vet who has chosen to spend his or her life time at the back end of a cow, either pulling something out or pushing something back in, rather than taking care of small insecure dogs like miniature French poodles who know how stupid they look and consequently hate everybody.

In exchange for their invaluable expertise the farmer learns to live with the idiosyncrasies of his local veterinarian. He knows that the vet, in the urgency of getting on to the next call to save a life, may occasionally forget a nose lead or a down jacket, but so far no vet has ever forgotten his truck.

Farmers wonder why, when the vet has to put an animal 'down', they know that the animal is going down. Most of them have led virtuous lives and may just go 'up' instead.

As we watch this walking encyclopedia of medical knowledge alternately thump, poke and listen to our sick cow, we have learned the meaning of some at the simplest technical terms used by all vets. For example, "Ummm" means "Oh, my God," "Uh huh" means "Good Lord," and

"Ah hah" means "I vaguely remember seeing a case like this in vet school but it hadn't advanced this far."

In spite of the odds against them, most of the time the vet saves the lives of my cows, using a combination of modern medicine, knowledge and hard won experience.

Yes, any dairy farmer who brags that they don't need the services of a veterinarian will lie about other things. too.

# THINGS I KNOW I'LL NEVER HEAR

We pretty much know what the people we work with are going to say in any given situation. Just once I would love to hear them say something different, something pleasing and, in reality, something impossible.

For example, my wife will never be able to say to me, "Why did you come in so soon? We don't have to leave for another hour." My loan officer will never be caught saying, "If things get too tight, just skip a few payments until things get better." A parts person will never be heard announcing, "I have everything you need on hand, and can even bring them out if you wish."

Just once I would like to hear a salesman proclaim, "Take your time. I'll hold this price until you make up your mind." Sadly, I will never hear my repairman utter, "Don't worry. I'll be there within the hour with everything I'll need to get you back in the field by noon."

Even though we receive excellent service from our A.I technician, he will never be heard stating, "No thanks, I don't need any help. I look upon breeding those wild and frisky ones as a challenge."

A milk truck driver will never declare, "Don't bother sanding your driveway. I need to learn how to drive one of these things on glare ice anyway." I don't think I'll ever hear my veterinarian remark, "You were right. I always learn something from you every time I come here."

You will never hear a farm supply route driver remark, "I hope you don't need much today. I'm running

late and didn't take time to restock my truck this morning."
I can't imagine a carpenter ever declaring, "You can make as
many changes as you want as we go along; it won't cost any
extra."

I would love to hear a fuel delivery person
pronounce, "I left the price per gallon blank on your
delivery slip; just fill in whatever price you want." I will
never hear my cooperative extension agent declare, "That's
easy. I knew the answer to that question without even
looking it up."

I'll know I am living in a fantasy world if I ever
expect to hear those words from my favorite people. I just
hope I live long enough to hear one of my neighbors, new to
the rigors of country life, say, "And don't worry about a little
manure spilled in the road." It will make it easier to find my
car in the company parking lot tomorrow."

# THOSE DREADED WORDS

There is one phrase that can strike fear and dread into the heart of the toughest dairy farmer. Just say, "The federal inspector is coming" and you will see a great flurry of activity as brooms and scrub brushes fly in all directions.

Why, when the quality of milk on all dairy farms is monitored very closely? Milk samples are taken and tested frequently. If any quality problems should occur they are addressed and remedied immediately. They have to be or the farmers would not be able to sell milk any more. It is a great system. The public is assured of a consistent supply of a high quality product at a reasonable cost and the farmer has a reliable market for the milk he produces.

If this is the way it is, why so much fear of the federal inspector? Well, the federal government requires all dairy farms to pass a stringent inspection with at least a score of 90 or better to be able to sell milk in interstate markets. Since the quality of milk is already assured, the federal inspector seems to show an over-riding concern for spider webs and fly specks.

Every organization, cooperative or company that buys milk from farmers has a field person who must prod, cajole and implore all their farmers to be ready at all times for a spot inspection from the dreaded "federal inspector." So, every time our field person calls with the dire message, "The federal inspector could come at any time," we frantically scrub every wall, wipe away every spider web and sweep every floor, only to never see anyone stop to admire our efforts.    That's because all federal inspections are "spot" inspections, meaning that not every farm is visited every time.   Nevertheless, we must all be ready at all times, just in case.

After one of these jarring calls, it occurred to me, as I stood precariously on a make shift stool scrubbing the milk house ceiling, that there really was no federal inspector.  All the field person needed to do was to call her farmers and breathlessly announce, "The federal inspector is coming."   She knew we would all spring into action cleaning everything in sight.   What a clever way to keep all her dairies clean and spotless in case the mythical federal inspector should ever appear.

# PHONE CALLS

Having a phone in the barn is certainly a great convenience for calling the breeder, vet or machinery dealer. However, incoming calls are another story.

Phone calls seem to come only at three times: when I am at the far end of the barn, when I am comfortably seated on the john with a good book, or when I have just let a group of cows out of the parlor and there are six slow, plodding bovines between me and the phone. The time that I do make it to the phone before someone hangs up, is usually a call for which I have no time or interest.

Being a polite person, I can't just hang up and go back to work. That would be rude. Instead, I am working on a sound effects machine to provide appropriate background noises to convince callers that I am simply too busy to take their call at that moment.

For example, for someone taking a survey, I will merely say, "I'm bleeding, but don't worry, an ambulance is on the way." Then they will hear a siren and quickly move on to the next name on their list. To impress reporters wanting to interview a modem, efficient, business-like farmer, I will have sounds of a computer whirring and clicking in the background.

For vacuum cleaner or insulated storm window salespeople who wish to make an appointment to come to my house, a push of a button will produce the blood curdling sound of a vicious, snarling police dog. For computerized calls about carpet cleaning, there will be a sound in code that will erase their entire program, reducing their computer to a smoldering pile of bits and bytes.

For lonely old ladies who confuse my number with that of their son who never calls, I'll have one button to produce a call-waiting signal. Bill collectors will hear the sound of a tow truck repossessing my car, to convince them to wait just two more weeks.

Owners of cellular phones need only one sound to keep their calls short and to the point, that of a grinding car crash followed by sirens. Most people hang up after that.

To get a machine like this, just call. Better let it ring, though, as I'll probably still be trying to get my pants zipped.

# I'VE HEARD THEM ALL!

Sometimes what someone tells you isn't necessarily what they mean. It isn't that they are intentionally devious or dishonest; they simply find it easier to tell you what you want to hear rather than tell you the truth. The challenge is telling the difference between truth and fantasy.

We have all heard the excuse for a late payment, "The check is in the mail," when we know that the check hasn't even been written. Some of the phrases I have heard are much more creative.

My mechanic will blithely say things like, "Go ahead and cut that field down. I should have your chopper running by noon." Translated, that means he still can't figure out what's wrong with it. My veterinarian will give me some very specific, finger-numbing, muscle-straining instructions over the phone and conclude by saying, "Then just twist, lift and pull, all at the same time, and the calf should come right out." That tells me that he is not very anxious to come out on a night like this to stand half-naked in a freezing barn just to do what you ought to be able to do yourself, providing you have the hands of a surgeon, the agility of a teenage gymnast and the strength of an Olympic wrestler.

The phrase I hate most to hear from a prospective customer is the dreaded words, "I want the best, price is no object." That usually means they are pompous, arrogant egomaniacs who, after the deal is struck, don't intend to pay. That is similar to the situation where someone will make you an attractive offer on the guise that they really care more about you than in making a profit.   When someone says they aren't in it for the money, believe me, they are in it for the money.

While the use of these high sounding excuses may be pleasing to the ear, what we really need is the blunt reality of truth. I'll know that time has come when the parts man at the John Deere dealership, instead of optimistically promising overnight delivery, just blurts out that he has no idea when my part will come.   Sometimes the truth hurts, but at least I'll know he is telling me "like it is."

# PARTS OF A FARMER

Are farmers really any different than everyone
else?  Do they possess some magical property that enables
them to juggle so many jobs all at once?  The superhuman
powers farmers seem to have are the culmination of
generations of man's struggles with nature, in the never-
ending battle between the human race and the elements.  A
farmer has evolved into a body with complex, clever and
comical parts.

A farmer needs the mind of a philosopher to
understand why a glass of milk in a restaurant for a dollar
is too expensive, but a glass of beer costing three dollars is
accepted without complaint.

He needs the eyes of superman to see and identify a
cow in heat in the dark when she stands two hundred feet
away.  A farmer must have the ears of a piano tuner to
distinguish between the clatter of a loose chain on a
machine and the barely audible squeak of a dry bearing.
And he needs the tongue of a Saint Bernard to lick the last
of the milk foam from his mustache.

A farmer requires the heart of Mother Theresa to
have so many beating hearts dependent on his every
decision.  He needs the arms of Sampson to lift the
burdens of deciding each day between what could be done
and what must be done.

He must have the stomach of an Eskimo to be able
to treat a bad case of foot rot, knowing he is going to have
hash for supper.  He needs the nose of a bloodhound to

distinguish between ketosis, metritis and Limburger. He requires the legs of an Olympic runner to outmaneuver a loose heifer in an icy barnyard and the knees of a weight lifter to handle all those bales, bags and buckets.

A farmer needs feet strong enough to stand on concrete all day and still be able to go bowling at night. He needs toes of a stone statue to take the daily stubbing, kicking and stepping upon.

Most importantly, he needs the shoulders of Atlas to bear the weight of the thought that, for most of the world's people, the farmer is the only thing standing between them and starvation.

# Chapter 9

## TIMES ARE CHANGING

Times are changing on the farm. As has happened for centuries, today's modern farms are again making their gradual transition from one generation to the next.

In this process each new family must learn to cope with the complexities of modern farm life. For example, most farmers, when asked where each variety of corn had been planted, will reply, "I had all that information written down in my little notebook, but it is gone now." Then, almost apologetically, they will say, "I left it in my shirt pocket and it went through the wash."

I was brought up by a mother who emptied my pockets on washday, no matter how dirty they were. Most farm women today work full time, both in and outside the home, and are not about to go searching through chaff-filled pockets for small notebooks, jackknives and other paraphernalia.

What changes will the next generation make? Well, as one young farmer said to me, "I wash all my own barn clothes now so I can get them done just the way I want."

Innocently, I asked, "How long have you been doing that?"

With a feeling of chagrin, he replied, "Since the second time my wife ran my pocket watch through the washer and dryer!

# COUNTY FAIRS

I love county fairs! They are an essential adjunct to summer in the country. 4-H and FFA members spend all summer anticipating them; tractor pullers stay up late preparing for them; mothers of teenagers lose sleep during them, and children of all ages live for them

A county fair is really a microcosm of rural life, where you might see a beaming grandmother with her blue ribbon quilt, a museum filled with early farm tools, or a first-time showman struggling with an unruly heifer, longing to return to the freedom of a lush and luxurious pasture.

On just a short stroll you might see a pitchman selling knives which he claims never need sharpening or a field full of old tractors, all restored to better than new condition, putt-putting their way to eternal life.

Fairs are beautiful cows and prize-winning sows, new tractors with air conditioned cabs (the envy of most farm dads), petting zoos and clowns with oversized shoes, new magicians and old traditions, farm machines and dairy queens, and kids of all sizes hugging panda bear prizes.

But the real reason I love fairs is the plethora of foods found there. A virtual cholesterol court of onion rings and sticky things, fried cakes and stomach aches, curly fries and homemade pies, all washed down with farm fresh milk.

You leave amidst the black diesel smoke hovering over the tractor pull, the screams of children riding the tilt-a-whirl and the tantalizing aroma of barbecuing chicken. You can't wait to come back next year. That's why I love county fairs.

# SIGNS

I am confused by all of those modern signs that use symbols instead of words to inform drivers of what's ahead. I yearn for the good old days when, approaching a farm, you would see a sign saying "Danger - slow moving vehicles ahead."

But of course, in those days, to graduate from high school, you had to be able to read. Today, since so few people can read, most traffic signs have been reduced to mere pictographs. Now, to warn you of slow moving traffic ahead, a sign bearing the silhouette of a man wearing a straw hat sitting on a tractor is used. To most drivers, this could either mean you are approaching a store that sells tractors or a farm museum featuring antique farm equipment. While the speeding motorist contemplates which meaning, he has probably skidded into the rear of a manure spreader. I mean, how much trouble would it be to put the words "slow moving vehicle" under the picture of the straw-hatted tractor driver?

The modern version of the old cattle crossing signs is even funnier. It is a picture of a Texas longhorn with an udder, an animal rarely seen on New York farms. I guess the NY Department of Transportation wanted to cover all possible situations. The two words "cattle crossing" under the cow silhouette couldn't cost very much and might save a motorist from suddenly acquiring a new, large and expensive hood ornament. Each time I see the sign that uses real words to say "deaf child area," I wonder why it hasn't been replaced with a picture of a child with no ears.

While we are at it, how about simply putting the short, almost impossible to misunderstand, words "men" and "women" on all restroom doors?  The present practice of using two identical stick figures to label restrooms brings new meaning to the term, "restroom roulette." I just go right in, and if no one screams, it must be the men's room.  Two small words would prevent those embarrassing times when I guess wrong.

Don't misunderstand me, I am not asking that we abandon all picture signs.  But if the intent of the sign is to inform, common sense would dictate the addition of a few words of explanation.  But then again, I wonder why we even use the term "common sense," because it really isn't all that common.

# I'M A KEEPER

As a keen observer of the human species, I have come to the conclusion that there are only two kinds of people, those who keep everything and those who don't. The throwawayers, also known as neatness freaks, keep only what they absolutely need and have a place for everything.  This is certainly an enviable trait, although somewhat dismaying to us keepers.

I have often wondered what it would be like to have a spotless, well-organized shop bench or a desk so free of clutter that you could actually see the entire desktop at once. Where do they put everything?  Is it stored away in properly labeled drawers?  Or perhaps on shelves, grouped by subject matter?

To us keepers, this is a sure sign of someone with entirely too much leisure time.  Either that, or they just don't have much stuff accumulated yet.

Keepers don't have to refer to indexes or charts to know where everything is.  We know whatever we want or need has got to be here somewhere, because we never throw anything away.  The trick is to remember which area of which building to rummage through to find what you are seeking.  We know, for example, that the chain saw is either in the milk house, shop, or still pinched in a felled tree. Extra fuses might be found in the shop, barn office, or under the seat of the car.

Whenever we replace anything, for any reason, we always keep the old one, just in case.  Right now I'm the proud possessor of boxes of old faucets, milker parts and broken mower guards. It's the kind of accumulation of pure junk that all auctioneers dread. Where do we keep all this stuff you may well ask? Simply put, it is everywhere! All over floors, on shelves, leaning against things and even under the dog. This easy accessibility is denied throwawayers, but that's the price that they pay for neatness.

Throwawayers may be neater, but us keepers have more fun!

# HAYING

Today haying seems so simple.  Just mow, chop, dump and pack, over and over and over.  It is so automatic, sometimes I feel like a robot.  It wasn't always this easy or fast.

You see, I grew up harvesting loose hay.  This didn't mean the hay had loose morals, just that it was hauled from field to mow in loose fluffy loads.  Yes, this was before the days of field balers or forage harvesters that we now readily take for granted.

After the hay was mowed and windrowed we would straddle the windrows, towing a flat bed wagon and pulling a hay loader, an amazing machine which would gobble up each windrow and deliver the hay to a person on the wagon who would skillfully build, layer by layer, a straight-walled load, a near impossibility using something as slippery as mature timothy hay.  Surprisingly, that was the easy part.  Getting that load of hay into the mow was even harder.

The mow, for us, was the entire third level of our big cow barn, known affectionately as the new barn, even though it was built about 1870.  Large chunks of the load were lifted into the mow using a long, heavy hay rope, a large grappling fork, a system of pulleys, rails, and trolleys and one horse.  Horses were used because they were strong and economical, but mostly because they were quieter than a truck or tractor.  Silence was essential so the workers in the mow could communicate with the person on the load.  Remember, this was before two-way radios.  As each

portion of hay was lifted into the mow, a trip rope held by
the person on the load could be yanked on a signal from the
mow and the large pile of hay would fall and land exactly
between two mow beams and be forked back against the
outside walls of the barn.  Known as "mowing away the
hay," this was hot and dusty work in a mow with little air
circulation.  If the load was tripped at the wrong time and
landed on a beam, spurts of profanity could be heard from
the mow.

My job was to drive the tractor in the field and the
horse at the barn.  The horse, "Chubby," was not known
for his ambition or originality but, unlike some farmhands,
he could follow directions, stoically and cheerfully.  The
rope that lifted all of this hay broke occasionally, usually
at the most inopportune times, resulting in more profanity.
The rope was repaired by making a long, woven splice
smooth enough to pass through large wooden pulleys.  Just
tying a knot wouldn't do.  The hour it took my father to
splice a hay rope was, to us, an all too brief respite from
the hot, dusty work of haying.  To my father, it was
another hour lost from harvesting our winter feed supply.
Adults and children never look at these events the same
way.  Today haying may be faster, but there's more to
break than just the hay rope.

## GO GET THE HORSES IN

It hardly seems like 50 years ago that those dreaded words from my father's lips struck fear into my 11-year-old heart. It meant time to rake hay with our mismatched team of Dexter and Chubby. Dexter was headstrong, a born leader, while Chubby was a meek, complacent old horse who let you make all the decisions for him.

The pair was always pastured in an almost square twelve-acre field of marsh grass and wild apple trees. They had to be driven into the corner of the field, up a lane to the barnyard and into the horse stable where my father would harness them.

Sounds easy, doesn't it?  The problem was that they knew whenever they saw my brother and me coming it meant several hours of sweaty hard work for them, so they would turn and run, trying to elude us. After several trips around the outside edge of the pasture, we usually tricked them into the lane.  From then on we had the upper hand, as long as we remembered to close the lane gate.  At this point they sensed defeat and meekly ran into the horse stable. as if to impress us with their submissiveness.

Now when I want to rake hay all I have to do is turn the key, listen to the diesel engine roar to life and back up to the rake.  I still think of Dexter and Chubby every time I do it, but only for an instant.  Then I turn up the radio and forget all about them again.

# I LOVE APPLES

I love apples, especially the big juicy ones plucked fresh from the tree. It all seems so easy to just reach up, twist slightly and suddenly in your hands is the most delicious fruit known to man. It will be nearly perfect, without blemishes, traces of disease or wormholes, just as God intended. Well, maybe, for you see that perfect apple is the result of generations of breeding and cultural development by farmers, university researchers and chemical companies. Unfortunately, if God had that tree all to himself, that apple would not be as large, tasty or disease free. Most people don't appreciate this miracle, but I do.

Growing up on a dairy and fruit farm, I helped my father prune, spray and care for 14 acres of apples. They were proud old trees with stately names like Golden Russet, Red Astrachan and Yellow Transparent. Almost weekly, from April to August, we sprayed those trees from crown to root, with those early pesticides like malathion, arsenate of lead and, of course, DDT. We did this with an old Meyers piston pump sprayer that built up 500 pounds pressure, pulled by our old faithful 1937 unstyled John Deere A. Standing on top of the sprayer's wooden tank, my father wielded this man-killer of a high pressure hose, as if fighting a huge fish on the end of a line, and thoroughly saturated these mammoth trees with a 60 foot long stream of spray. Meanwhile I deftly guided the old A at 2½ mph from tree to tree, my denim-clad body dripping with poisons from the spray's drift. I often think that if DDT were as poisonous as some say it is, I would have lost most of my hair by now.

In caring for an orchard the work never ended. In winter trunks were wrapped with hardware cloth to protect them from hungry rabbits; in spring trees were hand fertilized; and in the summer the entire orchard was mowed. Winter was also the time to prune trees, removing all the new shoots or suckers, cutting out any dead limbs and generally letting light into the inside of the trees. In the spring, when we weren't spraying or fertilizing, we picked up brush with a fence-wire brush boat for burning later. In the fall we picked apples into pails and carefully poured those pails into boxes which were drawn to the house and carried one by one down into our cavernous cellar and stacked, to be sorted later.

Each evening all winter, after a full day of dairy farming, my parents would go down cellar and slowly and carefully hand sort all of those boxes into different grades. All that work to find those few perfect apples that we now so effortlessly grab as a snack on our way to aerobics class. Believe me, if you had grown those apples, you would be too tired to even think about aerobics.

# BENT NAILS

All my life I have been driving old nails out of junk lumber, neatly stacking the lumber for future use and saving the nails in cans, jars and boxes. Why? Well, I recently asked myself that very question. I rarely use any of my horde of used boards. As for the tons of bent nails I have accumulated, they certainly are safe in my possession.

Have you ever straightened a bent nail and then tried to drive it again? First, there is the finger-smashing job of holding the bent nail with the "hump" up so it can be pounded just straight to bring it close to perfection, then rolling it on a flat surface to find the high spot, and hitting it again.

Even if you do get it straight, the head will never sit level enough to drive it with one good, solid blow from one direction. Instead, driving a previously bent nail involves skill, accuracy and the agility of an acrobat since with each stroke the nail must be attacked from another direction as it spirals itself into the wood. After all that effort and pain, using brand new nails seems too good to be true. I don't afford myself very many luxuries, but using brand new nails is one of them.

If that is the case, I'll bet you are wondering why I still save both the lumber and the nails from every building demolition project. Habit, I guess. My brothers and I were raised by hard-working, loving parents who met, married, set up housekeeping and started a family during the worst economic conditions of the twentieth century. One way we survived was to never buy anything new. Well, clothes perhaps, but not very often. We learned to take good care of what we had because we knew it had to last. Growing up, I never remember buying any lumber new. Every building project on the farm was done with recycled timber and often with used, formerly bent nails. We didn't do it that way because we were cheap or stingy, but because we had to. There was no other way.

That's why our generation enjoys such foolish and frivolous extravagances as eating out often, buying and enjoying gadgets like computers and electric pencil sharpeners and, yes, using brand new lumber and nails.

# GROWING OLD

When I was young, ten or so, I thought that my father was ancient. Somewhat of an oral historian, he often would regale our dinnertime conversations with tales that happened 20, 30 or even 40 years ago. To a child, anything earlier than yesterday was indeed ancient history. Now I am at the point where, at a moment's notice, I can bore young people of any age with stories from my past that I am sure sound like stories about the Civil War to them.

Could it be that I am indeed getting "old"? Yes, all of a sudden I realized that I have been farming over 35 years, attended over 2,000 calvings and was late for over 6,000 meals.

How does a farmer know when he is getting "old"? It's easy. Certain omens appear. For example, you may be visiting an agricultural museum and see on display a milking unit just like the one you had when you started farming. As you mentally reminisce about the many times you slid it under a cow, you notice a sign beneath it that says, "Early milking machine." That's an omen.

Or you notice that the six-acre cornfield that used to take all spring to plant now takes only a few hours to till and plant. Or you are amazed that cows today produce twice as much milk per day as cows did nearly 40 years ago. Older people tend to resist change whereas youth desire change in order to improve and move forward. Getting old isn't so bad if one can accept the changes necessary to remain competitive and successful.

Change is not easy, especially for someone like me who started farming without computers, mixer wagons and microwaves. Still, I am willing to cope with satellites, digital scales and even VCR's as long as milk cans, loose hay and bucket milkers are out of my life forever.

The good news is that my first tractor has become the favorite of restorers of antique farm equipment, which makes me an expert on vintage two cylinder tractors. I guess being ancient isn't so bad after all.

# EXPERIENCE

To the young, confidence is more important than experience. To the more mature, experience is more important than education.

On the farm, experience tells us to always slow down as we approach the manure push off, to never rake hay against the wind and to always clean a paintbrush the same day you use it. Sometimes experience is gained at a great cost. Too late we have learned never to chop the steepest part of a field when the grass is wet, never to chase heifers in the dark and never ever back up a truck with only one mirror.

Too often the value of experience is underrated. After all, experience makes us what we are. It's what separates the novice from the seasoned veteran. An optimist is a farmer who starts a new employee baling on a steep hill; a pessimist is one who won't. A cynic is one who did.

Only by experience will you learn never to plant corn in the dark, assume that a cow won't kick nor let a machine know that you are in a hurry. Painfully, I have learned to always make sure that the valve on the bulk tank is closed before starting to milk, to ask for a tow before the mud reaches the drawbar on the tractor, and to always spread manure into the wind.

Some of the valuable lessons I have learned from experience include: never get too close to an electric fence, never try to break a wheel nut loose with an open-end wrench, and never assume, even for a minute, that a cow won't notice that a gate has been left open. Experience has taught me to never use logic when arguing with a woman. Simply agree with her and then go ahead and do what you were going to do anyway. As valuable as experience is, in reality experience merely teaches us to recognize a mistake when we've made it again!

# EIGHT SECONDS OF GLORY

A strange car drove in as I finished filling the last free stall with sand. "Not another salesman," I cursed, proud of myself for finishing up on time. Then I saw an old friend emerge from the car looking distressed. He ran toward me, rambling on about how an "I Love NY" commercial was being filmed in town and his son was helping to find locations and extras for a NYC production company. They were in desperate need of someone to be a farmer in a commercial to be filmed the next morning. My friend made the bold suggestion that they use a real farmer and mentioned me. The director agreed but said, "We must see him first to be sure he fits our perception of a farmer."

Curious, I agreed to have them look me over and asked, "Do you want me to come as I am or do I have a few minutes to change?" One look at my cow-manure encrusted jeans and sweaty shirt lead my friend to comment, "You may come like that if you want to, but you are not riding in my car."

After receiving favorable reviews from the director that I did indeed look like a farmer, an appointment was made for early the next morning at the site of the filming. As promised, I appeared wearing my best bib overalls, plaid shirt and straw hat, trying my best to look like a farmer should. These urban experts found my denims too blue, my plaid shirt too distracting and my straw hat too something or other. Instead, they dressed me in faded overalls, a plain shirt with a long-john neckline and a more sedate straw hat. My sole role was to sit in a chair on the porch of a small town general store, reading a newspaper, blending into the background, and providing local color for a sequence that lasted not quite nine seconds. They shot and re-shot that same sequence with several variations until I nearly froze in that position.

This commercial should air next summer. I look forward to seeing this clip, even though very few farmers today wear bib overalls, long john tops and straw hats. And no farmer can afford to waste a morning sitting around reading the paper! But I can watch it confidently, knowing that I'm not just a farmer, I played one on TV.

# DAD'S PHILOSOPHY

Too often one's opinion of their father goes from a childlike, "My Daddy knows everything" to a teenager saying, "My Dad is so old fashioned" to a more mature, "I'll have to ask Dad about this, he's had so much experience," and then, sadly, to, "I wish Dad were around so I could talk this over with him."

My father, a lifelong farmer, had developed his own philosophy in order to survive the joys, hardships and heartbreaks of his chosen profession. For example, as a child, I complained bitterly about having to leave a family party early one Sunday afternoon to go home and milk the cows. My father, on the other hand, looked at the situation more philosophically. In his quiet way he pointed out that while there were times that it was disappointing to have to leave a good time for the drudgery of doing the necessary chores at home, there were also many times the responsibility of having to go home to milk was a good excuse to get away. He had come to accept the rigorous discipline required of all farmers as merely a way to quietly excuse himself from a too often boring situation and go back to the safe and secure routine in which we so often bury ourselves.

Other times, while growing up, I can remember when I turned to my father for advice with what I thought was a difficult decision. He must have figured that I would survive either way and he knew I was the one who had to live with those decisions, so he would remain noncommittal and utter those dreaded words, "You will have to use your own judgment." That was not the answer I desired. I wanted someone to take the burden of difficult decision-making from my shoulders. I will have to admit that now that I'm a father, reluctant to make decisions for others, I have come to love that phrase, "Use your own judgment."

It appears that one thing my father taught me was that being philosophical makes it easier to take on the rigors of everyday life. I'd like to reminisce more, but I've got to go milk.

# Order Form

**Peckhaven Publishing
178 Wagman's Ridge
Saratoga Springs NY 12866-6620**

Please send _____ copies of:

**A Cow In The Pool & Udder Humorous Farm Stories** to:

Name: _____

Address: _____

City: _____ State _____ Zip _____

Price: $14.95 each

Sales Tax: New York State orders please include 7% sales tax.

Shipping/Handling: $3.00 for the first book, $2.00 for each additional book.

Please remit in check or money order, payable to:
**Peckhaven Publishing**

Total amount enclosed: _____